# TELL ME WHY #2

BY ARKADY LEOKUM

ILLUSTRATIONS BY HOWARD BENDER

GROSSET & DUNLAP • New York

# CONTENTS

## Chapter 3
### The Human Body

## Chapter 4
### How Things Began

## Chapter 5
## How Things Are Made

# TELL ME WHY #2

# CHAPTER 1
# OUR WORLD

The moon doesn't look as if it's very far away, but its distance from the earth averages 239,000 miles. The diameter of the moon is 2,160 miles, or less than the distance across the United States. But when the moon is observed with a very large telescope, it looks as if it were only about 200 miles away.

## WHY DOES THE MOON FOLLOW US WHEN WE DRIVE?

Because the moon seems so close and big to us, we sometimes forget that 239,000 miles is quite a distance away. It is this great distance that explains why the moon seems to follow us when we drive in an automobile and look up at it.

To begin with, our feeling that this is happening is just that—only a feeling, a psychological reaction. When we speed along a road, we notice that everything moves past us. Trees, houses, fences, the road—all fly past us in the opposite direction.

Now there's the moon, part of what we see as we look out, and we naturally expect it also to be flying past us, or at least to be moving backward as we speed ahead. When this doesn't happen, we have the sensation that it is "following" us.

But why doesn't it happen? Because the distance of the moon from the earth is quite great. Compared to the distance our automobile travels in a few minutes, that distance is enormous. So as our automobile moves along, the angle at which we see the moon hardly changes.

In fact, we could go along a straight path for miles and the angle at which we would see the moon would still be basically the same. And as we notice everything else flying past, we get that feeling of the moon "following" us.

While we can't fully explain light, we can measure it quite accurately. We have a pretty good idea of how fast light travels. Since a light-year is merely the distance that a beam of light will travel in a year, the real discovery had to do with measuring the speed of light.

## HOW WAS THE LIGHT-YEAR DISCOVERED?

This was done by a Danish astronomer named Olaus Roemer in 1676. He noticed that the eclipses of one of the moons of Jupiter kept coming later and later as the earth moved in its orbit to the opposite side of the sun from that occupied by Jupiter. Then, as the earth moved back into its former position, the eclipses came on schedule again.

The difference in time added up to nearly 17 minutes. This could mean only that it takes that length of time for light to travel the diameter of the earth's orbit. This distance was known to be very nearly 186,000,000 miles. Since it took light about 1,000 seconds (nearly 17 minutes) to go this distance, it meant that the speed of light is about 186,000 miles per second.

In our own time, Professor Albert Michelson spent years trying to determine the exact speed of light. Using another method, he arrived at a speed of 186,284 miles per second, and this is now considered quite accurate.

If we multiply this speed by the seconds in a year, we find that light travels 5,880,000,000,000 miles in a year — and this is called a light-year.

---

Thousands of years ago, astronomers probably used the pyramids in Egypt and the towers and temples in Babylonia to help them study the sun, moon, and stars. There were no telescopes then. In time, astronomical instruments were developed, and as they became larger and more numerous, observatories were built to house them. Some observatories were built more than a thousand years ago.

## WHAT IS AN OBSERVATORY?

An observatory has to be built in the right place, a place with favorable weather conditions, moderate temperatures, many days of sunshine and nights without clouds, and as little haze, rain, and snow as possible. It must also be away from city lights and neon signs, which make the sky too light for good observation.

7

There are buildings which include living quarters in addition to telescopes. The instruments are housed in structures of steel and concrete. The building for the telescope is constructed in two parts. The lower part is stationary, and the upper part, or roof, is in the shape of a dome which can be rotated.

The dome has a "slit" which opens to permit the telescope to look out toward the sky. By rotating the dome on a track, the slit can be opened to any part of the sky. Both the dome and the telescope are moved by electric motors. In a modern observatory the astronomer only has to punch a number of buttons to move the equipment.

Of course, in order to see, the astronomer must always be near the eyepiece of the telescope or the camera attached to it. So, in some observatories the floor can be raised or lowered, or there is an adjustable platform.

Astronomers don't depend on their eyes alone to observe the skies. They have many complicated instruments and attachments to the telescope, such as cameras, spectroscopes, spectrographs, and spectroheliographs, all of which provide them with important information.

The discovery of things in the heavens often comes about much like the solving of a mystery. This is the way the asteroids were discovered.

Two men, Titius and Bode, had at different times figured out that

## WHAT IS AN ASTEROID?

there must be a planet between Mars and Jupiter; there was such a large gap in the distance between them. So several astronomers set about searching for this planet.

In 1801, a planet was actually found there. It was named Ceres, but is was a very tiny planet indeed, with a diameter of only 480 miles. So it was believed that it could be only one of a group of small planets and the search went on.

In time, three more tiny planets were found, the brightest of which was only half the size of Ceres. Astronomers decided that a larger planet must have exploded and left these four tiny pieces. But after 15 years of searching, another astronomer found still another tiny planet and this started the hunt again.

By 1890, 300 small planets had been found, and between 1890 and 1927, 2,000 had been discovered! These tiny planets, all rotating around the sun in the area between Mars and Jupiter, are called asteroids.

To indicate how small they are, 195 of them have diameters of more than 61 miles; 502, between 25 and 61 miles; 193, between 10 and 25 miles; and 22 of them have diameters of less than 10 miles!

If the mass of all the asteroids were added together, it would only be 1/3000 of that of the earth. So even if all the asteroids were united, they would form an insignificant planet.

As to how the asteroids were formed, the theory is that a satellite of Jupiter exploded and created these fragments.

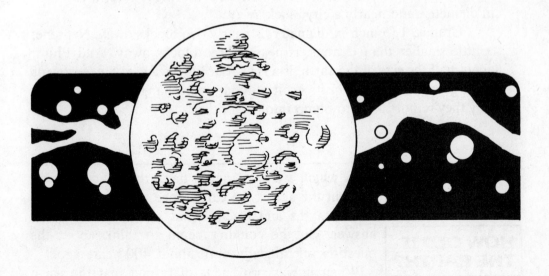

When we look up and see the stars and planets filling the sky, we might wonder if there might not be a collision up there some day. But luckily, this is not likely to happen.

## COULD THERE BE A COLLISION OF THE PLANETS?

What we don't realize when we look up is how much farther away certain stars and planets are from the earth than others. To get a better idea of this, let's consider our solar system and its planets. The planets never escape from the pull or attraction of the sun. They keep on moving around it in orbits that are not quite circles. Their speeds depend on their distances from the sun.

So let's start by imagining that your own head is the sun, both in its size and location in the solar system. Your head is then in the center of a number of rings of different sizes. These rings are the orbits which the planets travel around the sun.

With your head as the center, Mercury, revolving in the nearest ring, is 20 feet away from you! It is about as large as the dot at the end of this sentence. (Remember, the size of your head is the size of the sun.) Venus moves around in the second ring 39 feet away, and is about the size of the letter "o." In the third ring is our own planet, earth, a bit larger than Venus. It is 54 feet from your head (actually 93,000,000 miles away from the sun).

In the fourth ring is Mars, smaller than the earth, and 82 feet away. Next we come to Jupiter, the largest of all the planets. In relation to your head (the sun) it looks like a marble, and is as far from your head as the length of a football field! On the sixth ring is Saturn, 1/2 inch in diameter, and nearly a city block away.

Uranus, 1/5 inch in diameter, is nearly two blocks away. Neptune, a little smaller than Uranus, is nearly three blocks away. And Pluto, about half the size of the earth, is nearly four blocks away! Since each of them goes around you in its orbit without ever changing, you can see why they're not likely to bump into each other!

This is a question to which we may never have the exact answer. Man has wondered about the age of the earth since ancient times, and there were all kinds of myths and legends that seemed to have the answer. But he couldn't begin to think about the question scientifically until about 400 years ago.

## HOW OLD IS THE EARTH?

When it was proven at that time that the earth

revolved around the sun (in other words, that the earth was part of our solar system), then scientists knew where to begin. To find the age of the earth, it was necessary to explain how the solar system was born. How did the sun and all the planets come into being?

One theory was called the nebular hypothesis. According to this theory, there was once a great mass of white-hot gas whirling about in space and getting smaller and hotter all the time. As the gas cloud grew smaller, it threw off rings of gas. Each of these rings condensed to form a planet, and the rest of the mass shrank into the center to become the sun.

Another explanation is called the planetesimal theory. According to this, millions and millions of years ago, there was a huge mass made up of small, solid bodies called planetesimals, with the sun at the center. A great star came along and pulled on the sun so that parts of it broke away. These parts picked up the tiny planetesimals the way a rolling snowball picks up snow, and they became planets.

Whichever theory is right, astronomers have figured out that it all probably happened about 5,500,000,000 years ago! But other scientists besides astronomers have tackled this question. They tried to find the answer by studying how long it took for the earth to become the way we know it. They studied the length of time it takes to wear down the oldest mountains, or the time needed for the oceans to collect the salt they now contain.

After all their studies, these scientists agree with the astronomers: The earth is about 5,500,000,000 years old!

---

Take a look at a map of the world. Now look at the two continents of South America and Africa. Do you notice how South America sticks out to the right where Brazil is, and how Africa is indented on the left

## WERE THE CONTINENTS EVER JOINED TOGETHER?

side? Doesn't it seem as if you could fit them together like a puzzle and make them one continent?

Well, 50 years ago a German scientist named Alfred Wegener was doing just that. He wrote: "He who examines the opposite coasts of the South Atlantic Ocean must be somewhat surprised by the similarity of the shapes of the coastlines of Brazil and Africa. Every projection on the Brazilian side corresponds to a similarly shaped indentation on the African side."

Wegener also learned that naturalists had been studying the prehistoric plant and animal life of South America and Africa and had found many similarities. This convinced him that these two continents were once attached and had drifted apart.

He formulated a theory which he called the theory of the displacement of continents. According to this theory, the land masses of the earth were once all joined together in one continuous continent. There were rivers, lakes, and inland seas. Then for some unknown reason, this land mass began to break up. South America split off from Africa and drifted away. North America split off from Western Europe and floated to the west. All of the continents as we now know them were thus formed.

Did this actually happen as Wegener says it did? We don't know. It's only a theory. But as you can see from the map, there is some evidence to support it. And the study of prehistoric plant and animal life makes it seem possible, too. Besides, the earth's crust is still shifting today. So perhaps Wegener was right!

---

## WHY IS THE WATER FROM A GEYSER HOT?

Even if a geyser didn't shoot great streams of water into the air, it would be one of the most interesting marvels of nature. A geyser is really a hot spring, and a hot spring itself is quite amazing. Here is a hole in the ground filled with hot water. Where does the water come from? Why is it hot? And what makes it shoot up into the air if it's a geyser?

In all geysers, a hole called a tube leads from the surface to underground reservoirs which serve as storage basins for the water. Most of the water comes from rain and snow.

Deeper in the earth, the rock is very hot. This is probably uncooled lava, which is called magma. Gases from these hot rocks, mostly steam, rise through cracks in the rock and reach the underground reservoirs. They heat the water there to boiling and above-boiling temperatures.

This is how a hot spring is created. Now what makes it a geyser? The tube, or passageway from the water to the hot rocks below (where the heat comes from), does not go straight down in a geyser. It is twisted and irregular. This interferes with the natural rise of steam to the surface. If the steam and water can rise freely from below, we have a steadily-boiling hot spring.

The geyser erupts because the water in the irregular, or trapped, section of the underground water system is heated to the boiling point and suddenly turns to steam.

Steam requires more room than the water from which it was formed. So it pushes up the column of water above it. As this steam moves up, it lowers the pressure below, and more water turns into steam. Instead of there just being an overflow at the surface, there is a violent eruption as a result of the steam bursting upward, and we have the spectacle of a geyser!

Have you ever flown through clouds in an airplane, or perhaps been high up on a mountain where the clouds swirled all about you? Then you must have gotten a pretty good idea of what a cloud is: just an accumulation of mist.

## WHY DON'T ALL CLOUDS PRODUCE RAIN?

As you know, there is always water vapor in the air. During the summer there is more of this vapor in the air because the temperature is higher. When there is so much water vapor in the air that just a small reduction in temperature will make the vapor condense (form tiny droplets of water), we say the air is saturated.

It takes only a slight drop in temperature to make water vapor condense in saturated air. So when saturated warm air rises to an altitude where the temperature is lower, condensation takes place and we have a cloud. The molecules of water have come together to form countless little droplets.

What happens if all these water droplets in a cloud meet a mass of warm air? They evaporate—and the cloud disappears! This is why clouds are constantly changing shape. The water in them is changing back and forth from vapor to liquid.

The droplets of water in a cloud have weight, so gravity gradually pulls them down and they sink lower and lower. As most of them fall, they reach a warmer layer of air, and this warmer air causes them to evaporate. So here we have clouds that don't produce rain. They evaporate before the drops can reach the earth as rain.

But suppose the air beneath a cloud is not warmer air? Suppose it's very moist air? Naturally, the droplets won't evaporate. Instead, the droplets will get bigger and bigger as more and more condensation takes place.

Pretty soon, each tiny droplet has become a drop and it continues falling downward and we have rain!

---

Rainfall is now being measured in most parts of the world by means of an instrument called a rain gauge. The gauge of the United States Weather Bureau is shaped like a hollow tube closed at the lower end,

## HOW DO THEY MEASURE A RAINFALL?

with a funnel in the top.

This gauge is placed in an unsheltered place, and a graduated scale shows exactly how much rain has fallen in it. The Weather Bureau says that there has been an inch of rainfall if enough rain has fallen to make a sheet of water an inch deep over a given area.

A place having less than 10 inches of rainfall during the year is called a desert. Ten to 20 inches supports enough grass for grazing, while more than 20 inches is necessary for agriculture in most regions.

If more than 100 inches fall during the warm season, vegetation becomes so thick that cultivated plants are choked out. This is the case in the jungles of Brazil, in central Africa, and in India. There is a place in India, Cherrapunji, that gets about 450 inches of rainfall a year! By way of contrast, Egypt receives about one and one-half inches. In the United States, the coasts of Washington and Oregon get the most, about 80 to 100 inches. Parts of Arizona get less than three inches a year. Do you know what the average rainfall in your community is?

In an artesian well, the water can leap high into the air like a geyser from its prison far below the surface of the earth. The name comes from the Artois region in northern France where the first European well of

## WHAT IS AN ARTESIAN WELL?

this kind was drilled more than 800 years ago.

Artesian wells are possible only under certain conditions. There must be a layer of porous rock or sand that is buried between two layers of solid rock impervious to water. Somewhere this porous layer must be exposed to the surface so that water falling as rain or snow will sink downward until it is trapped between the solid, watertight layers above and below.

There the great pressure on all sides holds it prisoner until man releases it. When an opening only a few inches wide is bored straight down through the solid upper strata to the sandy layer, the freed water gushes to the surface with a mighty force.

The ancient Chinese and Egyptians dug artesian wells. Some of the older European wells required six or eight years to drill. Modern

**Artesian Well**

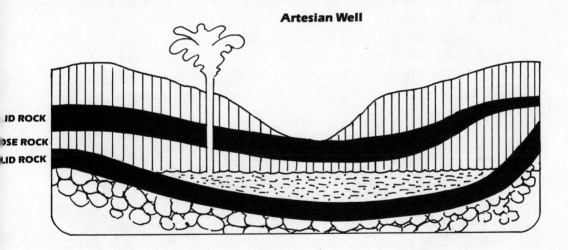

ID ROCK

OSE ROCK

LID ROCK

machinery makes drilling today a quick and simple task.

Near Edgemont, South Dakota, two wells drilled nearly 3,000 feet deep supply some 11,000,000 gallons daily. Coming from such a depth, this water registers a temperature of 100 degrees Fahrenheit when it reaches the surface. Another well in this region spouts even hotter water!

Several large cities in the United States, such as Pittsburgh, St. Louis, and Columbus, derive part, or all, of their water supply from artesian wells.

When a stream or river plunges over a wall of rock called a cliff or a precipice, we have a waterfall. If the waterfall is of great size, it is called a cataract. Where the rock wall is steeply slanted rather than

## WHAT MAKES A WATERFALL?

vertical, the rushing water is called a cascade. Sometimes in a cascade, the water descends in a whole series of steep slopes.

Niagara Falls is an example of how an overhanging rock ledge can create a waterfall. The upper layers of rock at Niagara are hard beds of dolomite. Below the dolomite is weak shale. The Niagara River plunges over the dolomite cliff into a great pool below, where the swirling water wears away the shale and thus undermines the dolomite above. From time to time, great masses of dolomite fall, keeping the cliff fresh and steep. In other waterfalls of this type, the hard rock may be sandstone, limestone, or lava.

Another type of waterfall is illustrated by Lower Yellowstone Falls. A huge mass of molten rock was squeezed up from below in ancient times. It hardened and later formed a wall in the path of the river's course.

In some cases, ancient glaciers cut deep into mountain valleys, leaving the sides as steep cliffs and precipices from which the waterfalls plunge down. In still other cases, high plateaus have been lifted by movements of the earth's surface and the streams plunge over their edges.

The three most famous cataracts in the world are Niagara Falls, Victoria Falls in the Zambesi River in Africa, and Iguassú Falls between Argentina, Brazil, and Paraguay. Of these three, Niagara Falls has the greatest volume of water.

The world's highest waterfall is Angel Falls in Venezuela, which plunges 3,300 feet down. This waterfall was first seen by Jimmy Angel from a plane in 1935, and was first visited in 1948.

Some waterfalls are very useful to man in providing power. The falls are used to generate the electricity man uses to run factories. About half the world's potential water power is in Africa, but most of it has not yet been developed.

---

Most of us think of air as being "nothing," but air is definitely "something," if it is matter made up of certain gases. A gas does not have a definite size or shape, but it takes up space.

## DOES THE AIR HAVE WEIGHT?

The great ocean of air that surrounds the earth and extends for many miles upward is attracted and held to the earth by gravity. Thus air has weight. And since air is everywhere about us, it adds weight to every object it fills. For example, there is a small amount of air in a volley ball. If you were to weigh two such balls, with the air let out of one of them, you would find it's lighter than the other.

The weight of air exerts pressure. The air presses on your whole body from all directions, just as the water would if you were at the bottom of the sea. The great mass of air pushes down on the earth very hard with a pressure of 14.7 pounds on each square inch, or roughly 15 pounds.

The 15 pounds is the weight of a column of air 1 inch square and as many miles high as the air extends upward. The palm of your hand has about 12 square inches. Imagine 15 x 12, or 180 pounds, all held up on one hand! The reason you don't even know you're doing this is that the air under your hand pushes up with the same force as the air above pushes down. There are about 600 pounds of air pressure on your head. But you're not mashed flat because there's air inside your body, too, which pushes out just as the air outside pushes in.

The higher up you go (to a mountain top, for example), the less air there is above you, so the pressure is less. At 20,000 feet, the pressure is only 6.4 pounds per square inch. At 10,000 feet, it's 10.16 pounds per square inch. If you could get up to 62 miles over the earth, there would be almost no pressure.

---

Would the world really be so much better off if there were no dust? The answer is: in some ways—yes; in some ways—no. What is dust, anyway? It consists of particles of earth, or other solid matter, which

## WHAT WOULD HAPPEN IF THERE WERE NO DUST?

are light enough to be raised and carried by the wind. Where do these particles come from? They might come from dead plant and animal matter, from sea salt, from desert or volcanic sand, and from ashes or soot.

For the most part, dust is not a very desirable or beneficial thing. But in one way, it helps make the world more beautiful! The lovely colors of the dawn and of twilight depend to a great extent on the amount of dust that is present in the air.

Particles of dust in the upper air reflect the sun's rays. This makes its light visible on earth an hour or two after sunset. The different colors which make up the sun's light are bent at different angles as they are reflected by the dust and water vapor particles. Sunsets are red because these particles bend the red rays of the sun in such a way that they are the last rays to disappear from view.

Another useful function of dust has to do with rain. The water vapor in the air would not become a liquid very readily if it did not have the dust particles serving as centers for each drop of water. Therefore, clouds, mist, fog, and rain are largely formed of an infinite number of moisture-laden particles of dust.

---

Fog, dew, and clouds are all related. In fact, just one change in the conditions—such as the presence or absence of air currents—could make the difference as to whether there will be fog, dew, or clouds. Let's see

## WHY IS THERE FOG OVER LAKES?

why this is so, and why fogs appear in certain places.

Fog particles are small, less than 1/25,000 of an inch in diameter. When you have a dense fog and can't see in front of you, it's because there may be as many as 20,000 of these particles in one cubic inch.

In order for fog to form, the moisture must leave the air and condense. This means it must be cooled in some way, because cooler air cannot hold as much moisture as warm air. When the air is cooled below a certain point, called the dew or saturation point, then fog starts to form.

Fog formation also requires that the cool air be mixed into warmer air by an air current. If you have still air, the cooling will take place only near the ground and you will have dew. When there are rapidly rising air currents, the cooling takes place high in the air and you have clouds. So the air currents that mix the cool air into the warmer air must be gentle in order to create fog.

One of the conditions in which this happens is when a mass of warm air passes over a cold land or a cold sea. Or it could be the opposite, with cold air passing over warm water. This last condition is what happens during early morning in the autumn near bodies of water such as lakes and ponds. The cold air and currents of warm air mix gently and you get those familiar fogs which seem to hang in mid-air over a body of water.

---

Have you ever been at a beach where at low tide you have to walk way out in the water just to get in up to your knees? Yet there are some places where you can hardly tell the difference between high and low tide.

## WHY DON'T ALL PLACES HAVE THE SAME TIDES?

The reason for this has nothing to do with the moon. Tides are caused by gravitation. Just as the earth pulls on the moon, so the moon attracts or pulls on the earth, but with much less force. The pull of the moon upon the earth draws the ocean waters nearest to it toward the moon as a broad swell, or wave. This produces high tide.

The water on the opposite side of the earth gets the least pull from the moon since it is farthest away, so it forms a bulge, too. So we have high tide on the side toward the moon and also on the side opposite the moon.

As the moon goes around the earth, these two high "heaps" of water and lower levels of water keep in about the same position on the earth's surface in relation to the moon. In fact, if the earth's surface were entirely covered with water, the rotation of high tides and low tides would be very regular.

But there are many things that interfere with this. One is the great bulk of the continents. They cause tidal currents which follow the shore-lines and pile up in certain places, such as bays.

On coasts that are gently sloping and straight, the incoming tide has room to spread out and may not rise very high. But where the incoming tide enters a narrow bay or channel, it cannot spread out, and the water may pile up to great heights. In the Bay of Fundy, for example, the difference between high and low tide may be more than 70 feet. Yet, in most of the Mediterranean Sea, the water rises only one or two feet at high tide.

---

Most winds, of course, don't have names. You just say, "It's windy," or "The wind is blowing." Sometimes we might say, "The north wind is blowing." But many of the winds do have special names.

## WHY DO WINDS HAVE DIFFERENT NAMES?

Those winds which have special names have acquired them for different reasons. For example, you know how it feels when you have the doldrums. You feel listless and without energy. Well, certain winds are actually called the doldrums! They are found near the equator where there is a great belt of rising air and low pressure. When you are caught in the doldrums in a ship, you are becalmed.

Winds that blow from above and below toward the equator are called the trade winds. Strong and steady, they got their names because in the days of sailing vessels they were a great help to navigation.

There are also some special winds. Monsoon winds, for example, are winds that change their direction with the season. In India, the monsoons blow south as hot, dry winds in the wintertime, and blow north in the summer, bringing heavy rainfall.

In southern France a cold, dry, northerly wind, the mistral, is dreaded by everyone. It blows steadily from the sea for days at a time and makes everybody irritable and uncomfortable!

On a windy day, it may seem to you that the wind is moving at tremendous speed. Then you hear the weather report, and it says, "Winds of 10 to 15 miles per hour." It's easy for us to be fooled about the speed

## HOW IS THE SPEED OF WIND MEASURED?

of the wind. But the exact wind speed is important to many people, so there are scientific ways of measuring the wind.

The first instrument for measuring the speed of the wind was invented in 1667 by an Englishman named Robert Hooke. The instrument is called an anemometer. There are many kinds of anemometers, but the most common type now used has a number of aluminum cups on a spindle. They are free to turn with the wind, and the harder the wind blows, the faster the cups will turn. By counting the number of turns made by the cups in a given time, the speed of the wind may be calculated.

When men began to fly, it was necessary to measure the winds at high altitudes. This was done by sending weather balloons up into the atmosphere and watching them with a special kind of telescope called a theodolite. But this wasn't much good when clouds hid the balloon. In 1941, weather radar was invented. And now a radar set can observe the balloon even through clouds and measure the winds in the upper air!

People have long been interested in knowing the direction of the wind. As long ago as A.D. 900, wind vanes were put on church steeples to show the direction of the wind!

Many a student who goes to college complains, "Why do I have to study physics and science, I'll never use these things." Of course, such people are quite wrong about "not using" physics and science. The fact

## WHY DOES ICE CRACK PIPES?

is that whether we know it or not, we all use the laws of physics in everyday life many, many times.

Any person who lives in a climate where it gets cold in winter, knows that he must put anti-freeze in the radiator of his car, and close off and empty any pipes that might have water in them. He knows that if he doesn't, the radiator will crack and the pipes might burst. The laws of physics explain why such things happen.

For example, when most substances change from a liquid to a solid state, they shrink. But exactly the opposite happens with water!

Instead of shrinking, it expands. And it doesn't expand by just any amount; it expands by about one ninth of its volume.

This means that if you start with nine quarts of water and this water freezes, you'll have 10 quarts of solid ice! Well, now just picture the water in an automobile radiator, or a pipe, freezing up. Ten quarts of ice need more room than nine quarts of water. But radiator pipes and water pipes can't stretch. There just isn't any more room. So when the water freezes, it makes more room for itself by cracking the pipes.

One of the amazing things about this process of nature, is the tremendous power it has. Pipes are made of pretty strong metals, as you know. In places like Finland, this power is actually put to work.

This is how they do it. In the quarries, they fill the cracks in the rock with water and allow it to freeze. The freezing water acts as a wedge and loosens the rock so that great blocks of rock are broken loose by the freezing power!

Even though ice takes up more space than water, it is lighter than water and floats upon it. This is the reason why large bodies of water never freeze solid. The sheet of ice on top protects the water beneath.

---

Even though stone and wooden houses have become more popular among the Eskimos, they still construct the igloo for special occasions or while on a journey. It is quickly built and it defies any kind of weather.

## WHY DOESN'T AN IGLOO MELT INSIDE?

First a trench is cut about 5 feet long and 20 inches deep in a newly made snowdrift. Then, from the face of the trench, blocks are cut with a knife. These are shaped so that they lean inward when set on edge.

A circle of these snowblocks is laid and then shaved down so that as the Eskimo builds there will be a narrowing spiral. The material is cut from the inside of the house as the man works. Then a keystone, with edges wider above than below, is dropped into the space at the top. Then all the cracks are filled in with soft snow. A small igloo can be built in this way in a couple of hours.

When the house has been built, the woman takes over. She lights her blubber lamp and makes it burn as hot as possible. Then she closes the door with a block of ice and makes everything airtight. Now the snow begins to melt. But because the dome's roof is curved, it doesn't drip. Instead, it soaks gradually into the blocks so that they are nearly wet through.

When the blocks are sufficiently wet, she puts out her lamp and opens the door. The intensely cold air rushes in, and in a few minutes, the house is transformed from a fragile building of snow to a dome of ice! It is now so strong that a polar bear can crawl over the roof without breaking it in. And because it is so solid and hard, it doesn't melt and provides a snug shelter.

Of course, when the winter ends and the temperature rises, the igloo does begin to melt, and it is usually the roof which first caves in.

---

Coral is one of the most curious and fascinating objects in the world! To begin with, red coral has been prized for jewelry since ancient times. But even more interesting is the amount of supersition that has existed concerning coral.

## WHAT IS CORAL?

Romans hung pieces of it around their children's necks to save them from danger. They believed it could prevent or cure diseases. In some parts of Italy, it is still worn to ward off "the evil eye." And most fascinating of all—coral has actually changed the geography of the world!

What is coral? It is the skeleton of the coral polyp, a tiny, jelly-like sea animal with many small tentacles. The polyp secretes a limey sub-

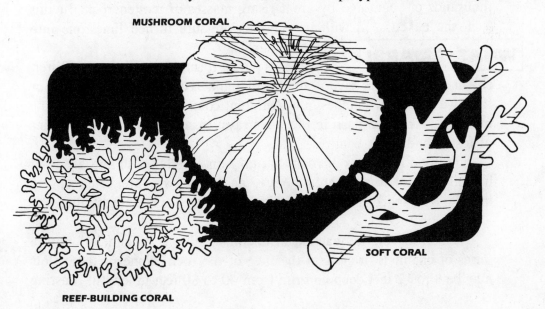

MUSHROOM CORAL

SOFT CORAL

REEF-BUILDING CORAL

stance of which the skeleton is composed. It is formed like a cup beneath and around the outside of the polyp.

The polyp first attaches itself to a rock beneath the surface of the water, and young polyp buds grow out from it. When the old polyp dies, the living polyps remain attached to its skeleton, and in their turn produce buds. Thus the process of building goes on as new generations of polyps rise above the skeletons of the old.

As layer upon layer of coral is built up, it actually forms reefs and islands in the ocean! These animals flourish in warm or tropical waters. Coral is found principally in the South Pacific, in the Indian Ocean, in the Mediterranean Sea, and in the waters off the coast of Florida, of Mexico, and of the West Indies.

The most important coral formations are called fringing reefs, barrier reefs, and atolls. Fringing reefs are underwater coral platforms attached to a body of land and extending into the ocean. Barrier reefs are not attached to the mainland but rise from the ocean at some distance from shore. And atolls are coral islands, shaped like a ring.

The Great Barrier Reef, which lies off Queensland, Australia, extends 1,260 miles to sea!

---

Nature is a master baker. Deep inside the earth is her oven, heated thousands of years ago by great rising masses of molten rock. In this oven she baked, and with tremendous pressure turned limestone into

## WHAT IS MARBLE?

hard marble.

In its purest form, marble is white. Different impurities often give it shades of pink, red, yellow, or brown, or form wavy lines or patches in it. Different colored crystals caught in the marble sparkle and flash in the sun's rays. In some marble the remains of fossils add to its beauty.

Many other kinds of rock that take on a high polish and are used in building, such as granite, onyx, and porphyry, are often called marble. Real marble, however, is limestone that has been crystallized by nature's process.

When marble is quarried a machine called a "channeler" cuts a series of channels or slots in the face of the rock. Some of these slots may be 8 to 12 feet deep and run from 60 to 80 feet in length. Blasting cannot be used because it would damage or shatter the marble. The blocks are lifted out carefully by large derricks.

A great toothless saw is set to work on the rough stone, while a stream of water containing sand is kept running over it. The friction of the steel blade and the sand soon cuts the marble into the desired sizes. Sometimes a wire saw is used instead of a solid blade.

Pieces of marble are then placed on a circular rubbing bed and held stationary. Sand and water flow over the rotating bed surface, rubbing away the marble to an even level. Then still more grinding is done to give it a smooth surface.

The last fine polishing is done by a mixture of tin oxide and oxalic acid applied to the surface of the marble by means of a buffer wheel.

---

The first records we have of people deliberately looking for diamonds indicate that this happened in India. Diamond mining as an industry started there more than 2,500 years ago!

## WERE DIAMONDS ALWAYS CONSIDERED VALUABLE?

Diamonds were prized from the very beginning. In fact, before the fifteenth century, diamonds were still so rare that only kings and queens owned them.

It was not until 1430 that the custom of wearing a diamond as a personal ornament was introduced. A lady named Agnes Sorel started the fashion in the French Court, and the custom spread throughout Europe. As a result, there was feverish activity in India for more than 300 years to supply diamonds.

Finally, this source became exhausted, and fortunately, diamonds were found on the other side of the world—in Brazil, in 1725. The jungle and tropical climate made conditions very difficult, but for more than 160 years, Brazil was the world's chief source of diamonds.

Today, the capital of the diamond empire is South Africa where, in 1867, important sources of diamonds were discovered by accident. A poor farmer's child found a pretty stone. A shrewd neighbor who recognized it as a gem diamond bought it, and when he sold it, diggers of all ages and nationalities flocked to the scene.

Within a year, three great diamond fields were found and the city of Kimberly, the center of a great diamond empire, was born.

The only difference between an industrial diamond and any other kind of diamond is that the industrial diamond is of an inferior grade. If it were of perfect quality, beautiful in color and without a flaw, the dia-

## WHAT IS AN INDUSTRIAL DIAMOND?

mond would, of course, be used in jewelry, where it brings higher prices.

It may seem astonishing to you that something as precious as a diamond is used in industry at all, but the diamond has been called the "emperor of industry!"

Our word "diamond" comes from the Greek word *adamas,* which means "unconquerable." A diamond is truly unconquerable, for nothing in the world can cut it—except another diamond!

So three fourths of all diamonds that are found don't go into jewelry at all. They are used in industry. And they are used because of their extreme hardness. For instance, about 20 per cent of all industrial diamonds are mounted in drills and used by mining companies to drill through rock.

Diamonds are crushed to dust and this diamond dust is used in making diamond-grinding wheels. These wheels sharpen certain tools and also grind lenses. Other diamonds are used in dies. Without diamonds, some of our most important industries would have to shut down.

Man discovered copper before any other metal except gold. Before the dawn of history, it was used by Stone Age men.

Copper is found in a fairly pure state, in lumps and grains of free

## WHAT IS COPPER?

metal. Probably men first picked up the lumps because they were pretty. Then they made the great discovery that these strange red stones could be beaten into any shape. This was an easier method of making weapons and knives than chipping away at flints.

Much later, other men discovered that they could melt the red stones and form the softened mass into cups and bowls. Then they started to mine for copper and to make all sorts of implements and utensils out of it.

For thousands of years, copper remained the only workable metal known, for gold was not only too scarce to be considered but also too soft to be practical. Copper tools were probably used in building the great Egyptian pyramids.

When bronze, an alloy of copper and tin, was discovered, still greater quantities of copper were mined. But after the discovery of iron, copper was little used, except among semi-civilized peoples, until the present age of electricity. Because copper is such a good conductor of electricity, it is a very important metal in modern industry.

Few people ever see pure copper or would recognize it if they did. It is a shining, silvery substance delicately tinted with pink that turns a deeper red when exposed to the air. The copper we generally see has a dull reddish-brown surface. This is an oxide formed when the metal combines with the oxygen of the air.

Most of the world's copper exists in combination with other substances from which it must be separated before it can be used. Often it is found combined with sulphur in what we call a sulphide ore. This sulphide ore may be combined with such substances as iron and arsenic and this makes the separation of the copper difficult.

Copper has many other virtues besides that of outlasting most other metals. It is tough, yet soft enough to be pulled and pounded and twisted into any shape. It is an excellent conductor of heat as well as of electricity. It can be carved or etched, but is not easily broken. And it can be combined with other metals to make such alloys as bronze and brass.

---

Nickel forms many alloys which are used in hundreds of industries in many ways. It is one of the most useful metals known to man. But in early times, when chemists first tried to work with it, it gave

## WHAT IS NICKEL?

them a great deal of trouble. In fact, the word nickel is derived from the German word for "imp!"

Nickel is found in meteorites, and it is sometimes found in the free state in small quantities. But the greatest supply of nickel is obtained from certain ores, especially one called pyrrhotite, which is a mineral containing iron, copper, and nickel. Canada is the greatest of all nickel-producing countries.

The ore containing nickel is usually heated in a blast furnace to obtain a rich mixture called a matte. This is then reduced to nickel by mixing it with coke and heating it in a blast furnace.

Nickel is silvery, lustrous, hard, and malleable, which means it can be easily worked and shaped. And nickel is one of the most magnetic materials known, unless heated.

We seldom see pure nickel except when it is used as a coating on other metals. This is then called nickel-plate. It protects other metals from rust or tarnish, and gives them a better wearing surface.

Most of the nickel produced is used in alloys, or in a mixture with other metals. For instance, when alloyed with copper, it is used in coins. Our own five-cent piece is called a nickel for that reason. When it is alloyed with three parts of copper and one of zinc, nickel forms a bright silvery metal known as German silver or nickel silver. This is used for making tableware and as a base for silverplated ware.

But these uses of nickel are relatively minor. Most nickel goes into the making of nickel steel, an alloy which can withstand repeated strains. It is used in structural work, bridges, railroad rails at curves, rivets, locomotive boilers, automobile gears and axles, and the dipper teeth of steam shovels.

---

Was there a time when there were no plants on earth? According to the theories of science, the answer is yes. Then, hundreds of millions of years ago, tiny specks of protoplasm appeared on earth. Protoplasm

## WHERE DID PLANTS COME FROM?

is the name for the living material that is found in both plants and animals. These original specks of protoplasms, according to scientists, were the beginnings of all our plants and animals.

The protoplasm specks that became plants developed thick walls and settled down to staying in one place. They also developed the green coloring matter known as chlorophyll which enabled them to make food from substances in the air, water, and soil.

These early green plants had only one cell, but later they formed groups of cells. Since they had no protection against drying out, they had to stay in the water. Today, some descendants of these original plants still survive, though they have changed quite a bit, of course. We call them algae. Seaweeds are an example of these plants.

One group of plants developed that obtained its food without the use of chloropyhll. These non-green plants are called the fungi, and they include bacteria, yeasts, molds, and mushrooms.

Most of the plants on earth today evolved from the algae. Certain of these came out of the sea and developed rootlets that could anchor

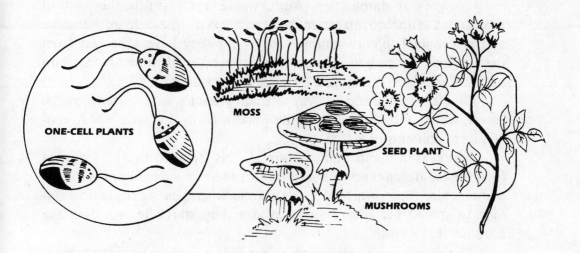

ONE-CELL PLANTS

MOSS

SEED PLANT

MUSHROOMS

them in the soil. They also developed little leaves with an outer skin covering as protection against drying. These plants became mosses and ferns.

All of the earliest plants reproduced either by simple cell division (as in the case of bacteria and yeast) or by means of spores. Spores are little dustlike cells something like seeds, but they contain no stored food in them as seeds do. As time went on, some of these plants developed flowers that produced true seeds.

Now we are pretty far advanced in the development of plants. Two different types of plants with seeds appeared; those with naked seeds and those with protected seeds. Each of these two types later developed along many different lines. In this way, we have traced the plants existing on the earth today back to an original speck of protoplasm that appeared long, long ago. At least, this is the theory of modern botanical science.

Is there anybody in your family on a diet? Then you've probably heard them say as they turned down a certain dish, "Not for me! Too much starch!" Of course, if there are growing children in a house, they are usually fed plenty of starch to "build them up."

## WHY DO PLANTS MAKE STARCH?

Starch—whether people try to cut down on it or to get all they can—is one of the most important substances in the world. The human race gets more food from starch than from any other single substance!

We get our starch from plants, where it is found in the form of tiny grains. How do plants make starch? With the help of sunshine and chlorophyll, plants combine the water they have absorbed from the soil and the carbon dioxide they have taken in from the air into sugar. This sugar is changed by plants into starch.

Plants store the starch away as small granules in their stems, roots, leaves, fruits, and seeds. The white potato, corn, rice, and wheat contain large amounts of starch.

The reason plants manufacture all this starch is that it serves as food for the development of seedlings or the new shoots until they can manufacture their own food materials. So when you see a plant beginning to spread out, you know that stored-up starch is providing the food for that growth.

For people and animals, starch supplies an energy-producing food. Like sugar, it is made up of carbon, hydrogen, and oxygen. It is not sweet; generally, it is tasteless. Certain chemical substances in the mouth, stomach, and intestines change the starchy food to grape sugar, which the body can use easily.

The way we get starch from the plant is to crush those parts of the plant where the starch is stored. The starch is washed out with water and allowed to settle to the bottom of large vats. The water is then squeezed out of the wet starch and the mass is dried and ground to a powder, which is the form in which starch is usually manufactured.

Starch has many unusual uses. It is used in laundering, as an adhesive, in the manufacture of cloth, and as the basis for many toilet preparations.

---

If a weak sugar solution is exposed to the air, in several days a light, frothy scum appears on the surface and the liquid begins to smell of alcohol. This change takes place because tiny plant cells called yeast

## WHAT IS YEAST?

have settled from the air into the liquid. They have found conditions favorable to their growth.

Man has long known that this process takes place and he has used it for thousands of years to make alcoholic beverages of all kinds. Sugar solutions made from molasses, potatoes, rye, corn, malt and hops, apples, and grapes have been exposed to the air to make alcohol, whiskey, beer, ale, cider, wine, and other beverages.

Probably through accident, it was also discovered that if bread dough were allowed to stand for some time before baking, very often a peculiar change took place. The flat lump of dough began mysteriously to swell and rise. It developed a strange but pleasant odor. When this dough was baked, instead of making a flat, heavy slab, it made a light, porous, soft bread!

In 1857, Louis Pasteur announced that he had discovered the explanation for these changes. He said they were due to the presence of tiny, one-celled plants called yeast. Yeasts belong to the fungi family, and are tiny, rounded, colorless bodies. They are larger than most bacteria, but still so small that it would take from 3,000 to 4,000 of them laid side by side to make an inch!

Yeast cells reproduce by budding. This means they send out projections which become cut off from the parent cell by a cell wall. Finally, these projections grow to full size. As they grow, they form substances called zymase and invertase.

These substances are called enzymes, and they have the power to ferment starch to sugar, and sugar to alcohol and carbon dioxide. As fermentation takes place, carbon dioxide is formed and rises to the top. Then it escapes, leaving the alcohol. Beer, ale, wine, and cider are fermented beverages in which yeast has changed some of the sugar to carbon dioxide and alcohol.

In breadmaking, the carbon dioxide collects in bubbles in the dough, which makes it rise. Heat later drives off the carbon dioxide, thus making the bread porous and light.

---

In millions of homes in Europe and the United States, the mistletoe is hung up at Christmastime. According to a happy custom, when a girl is standing under the mistletoe, a man is allowed to kiss her.

## WHAT IS MISTLETOE?

Curiously enough, the use of the mistletoe on holidays and ceremonial occasions goes back to quite ancient times. When the Romans invaded Britain and Gaul (now called France), the people who lived there were called Celts. These Celts were organized under a strong order of priests called Druids.

The Druids taught that the soul of man was immortal. Many of their rites were connected with the worship of trees, and they considered that whatever grew on a tree was a gift from heaven. Among the most sacred of these "gifts" was the mistletoe. They would cut the mistletoe with a golden knife and hang it over their doors to ward off evil spirits. According to them, only happiness could enter under the mistletoe. This was actually the beginning of the tradition of the kiss under the mistletoe!

Among the Scandinavian people, too, the mistletoe was considered lucky. They gathered it up during their winter festivals and each family received a bit of it to hang up over the entrance to their home. This was supposed to protect the family from evil spirits.

One reason the mistletoe came to be considered sacred is that it is a plant that has no roots in the earth. It grows on the branches of other trees. When the mistletoe is very young and just developing from a seed, it produces tiny outgrowths. These pierce the bark of the limb on which the seed fell. After they have grown through the bark to the wood, they spread out and in this way absorb a part of the moisture and the food which the tree contains.

The food and moisture go to nourish the young mistletoe plant, which then grows as most other plants do. So you see it has no direct connection with the soil and it doesn't need any! Sometimes, the mistletoe grows so abundantly it kills the tree that has given it life.

The mistletoe grows on oak and other kinds of trees in the southern and western United States. The berries which the plant produces are loved by birds. When they eat them, the sticky seeds cling to their beaks. In trying to remove them, the birds rub their beaks on other trees and so spread the seeds!

---

Can one kind of tree produce the fruit of another kind of tree?—Yes! Grafting makes it possible. If a bud from a twig of a pear tree is carefully inserted in a slit made in the bark of a quince bush, a pear twig

## WHAT IS GRAFTING?

will grow. The quince bush will bear both pears and quinces!

In the same way, an almond tree can be made to produce both peaches and almonds. Or a crab apple tree can be made to bear a crop of fine cultivated apples. Sometimes grafting is used to produce freak trees and bushes, but it has nevertheless an important place in agriculture.

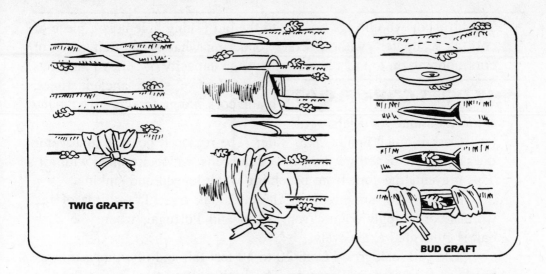

TWIG GRAFTS

BUD GRAFT

The first advantage of grafting is that it makes it possible for a nurseryman or gardener to be sure that his young trees or shrubs will bear the same quality and variety of fruit as the parent tree. A twig taken from a tree and grafted into another tree will produce the same type of fruit borne by the tree from which it was taken.

There are many methods of inserting the budded twigs, or scions, as they are called, into the stock of the other plant, but two rules must always be followed: First, only related species of trees or shrubs can be grafted. This means that apples can be grafted on pear and quince trees, and peaches can be grafted on apricot, almond, plum, or other stone fruit trees. But it is impossible to graft apples on peach trees, for example.

The second rule is that the cambium layer which carries the vital sap of the scion must touch the cambium layer of the stock on which it is grafted. Otherwise, the grafted twig cannot grow.

There are many different kinds of grafting. It can range from inserting a single bud under the bark to grafting long twigs across the wound of a tree in order to heal wide wounds in the bark.

Interestingly enough, grafting is being applied to animals, too. Eyes, for instance, have been replanted in such creatures as frogs, toads, rats, and rabbits. Surgeons have learned from these experiments how to help people who have been injured or disfigured. Bone taken from the ribs has actually been grafted onto the nasal bone to form a new nose, and skin has been grafted onto burnt tissue to remove scars!

The little boy who brings his line to the old fishing hole uses a piece of cork as a "floater" without ever wondering what keeps that piece of cork bobbing on top of the water. But the capacity of cork to float has

## WHY DOES CORK FLOAT?

been known since ancient times, and cork life-preservers saved many a life thousands of years ago!

Cork is much lighter than water. The reason it floats is that water does not easily penetrate the walls of the cells, which are filled with air. This prevents the cork from becoming water-logged and sinking.

Cork is the outer bark of the cork oak tree. Two-thirds of the world's cork supply comes from Spain and Portugal, where the cork oak is cultivated extensively.

The cork oak grows from 20 to 40 feet tall and often measures as much as four feet in diameter. The bark of this tree is usually first stripped when the tree is about 20 years old. This doesn't injure or kill the tree; instead, the stripping actually benefits it.

About nine years later, another stripping is taken. The cork obtained from these first two strippings is coarse and rough. Later strippings, which are made about nine years apart for about a hundred years, give cork of a finer quality.

After stripping, the cork is stacked for several weeks to season, and then boiled to soften it and to remove the tannic acid. After boiling, the cork lies in pliable flat sheets, which are dried and then packed for shipping all over the world.

There are two kinds of raw cork: One is known as corkwood. This is the material used to make cork stoppers, floats, and life preservers. The second kind of raw cork is called grinding cork. It is ground up and then baked, some of it with binder materials. This is made into pipe covering, shoe fillers, automobile gaskets, and liners such as you find in the crown of bottle covers.

One of the greatest uses of cork today is for soundproofing rooms, and for insulating warehouses, freezer rooms, and refrigerators.

Bamboo is one of the most phenomenal examples of plant life. It shoots upward at the rate of 16 inches a day. It may reach a height of 120 feet. It spreads so rapidly that if there is a road running through a growth

## WHAT IS BAMBOO?

of bamboo, that road may disappear completely in a month if it is not kept open!

There are about five hundred kinds of bamboos. They all have smooth, hollow, jointed stems with a strong, watertight partition at each joint, and all grow very rapidly. While most bamboos flower every year, there are some that bloom only three or four times in a century. The flowers are like those of grains and grasses. The fruit is usually like grain, and in some kinds, like nuts.

The bamboos are tropical and subtropical plants. They grow in Asia, in South America, and a few species grow in Africa. About thirty kinds of tall bamboos from other parts of the world have been successfully introduced into California and Florida.

The uses of bamboo are so numerous it is almost hard to believe. In the United States, bamboo is chiefly used in fishing poles, walking sticks, and phonograph needles. But it is in the Oriental countries that bamboo is really put to use.

People build entire houses with it, using large sections for posts and the split stems for rafters, roofing, and floor planks. They strip off the hard outer layers for mats and lattices to separate the rooms. The joints of the largest kinds are used for buckets and those of smaller ones for bottles.

There are even certain kinds of bamboos so hard that they can be made into crude knives, and beautiful and strong baskets are woven of strips from the outer coverings. In Japan, gardeners use hollowed bamboo stems for water pipes. In China, the inner pulp is made into the finer grades of native paper. The Javanese make bamboos into flutes. And many Oriental people eat the tender shoots of bamboo as a vegetable. So you see how valuable the bamboo is in certain parts of the world.

Amazingly enough, bamboo is a grass. It is the largest member of the family of grasses, though most people think of it as a bush or a tree.

---

The pomegranate is a fruit with a very interesting background in history. According to a legend of the ancient Greeks, the pomegranate was the fruit which Persephone ate while in Hades. Because she swallowed six of the seeds, she was forced to spend six months of each year in the underworld! To the Greeks, the juicy, many-seeded pomegranate always

## WHAT IS A POMEGRANATE?

symbolized the powers of darkness.

In China, the pomegranate was a symbol of fertility. King Solomon, according to the Bible, had an orchard of pomegranates. When the children of Israel wandered in the wilderness, they longed for the pomegranates they used to have in Egypt. Mohammed advised his followers, "Eat the pomegranate, for it purges the system of envy and hatred."

So you see the pomegranate was an important fruit in the East in ancient times. It is supposed to have originated in Persia, but from very ancient times, it has been grown in the warm countries of southern Asia, northern Africa, and southern Europe. Now it is common in South and Central America and in the southern United States.

The pomegranate grows as a bushy tree, or shrub. It grows from 5 to 20 feet high. Its leaves are glossy and at the ends of its slender twigs grow its coral-red, waxlike flowers.

The fruit is about the size of an orange. It is leathery-skinned and is colored a deep yellow, tinged with red. Inside this fruit are many small seeds. They are covered with a sweet, red, juicy pulp, which is often made into refreshing drinks. There is something about its taste that makes it especially agreeable to people who live in hot, dry regions.

There are many varieties of the pomegranate. In fact, a Moor who wrote about it 700 years ago described 10 different kinds which were grown in Spain at that time! In the United States, three leading varieties have been cultivated. They are called the Wonderful, the Paper-Shell, and the Spanish Ruby.

There is a difference between the Arctic Region and the Arctic Circle. The Arctic Circle goes around the northern part of the earth in a perfect circle, 66½ degrees north of the equator. At one time, the Arctic Region was considered to be all land and water lying north of this circle.

## DOES ANYTHING GROW IN THE ARCTIC REGION?

But today, the Arctic Region is considered to be a geographical unit based on the combination of a number of different elements, especially vegetation and climate. It extends south into Canada and includes all of Greenland.

The climate of the Arctic is not continuously cold, nor is the Arctic an area of heavy snow covered by ice. During the short, hot summer, temperatures may rise to 80 degrees Fahrenheit, and in some places, even reach 100 degrees. What makes the Arctic feel so cold is mainly the frequent, strong wind driving the dry crystals of snow before it.

Over much of the Arctic there are less than 15 inches of precipitation a year, although southern Greenland may have as much as 40 inches. As a result, a great number of plants grow in the Arctic. More than 1,300 different species of plants have been identified there, and more than half of them are of the flowering kind! Large areas are covered with moss and lichens, but in the southern regions of the Arctic, there are fertile valleys and grasslands.

Animals are quite numerous in the Arctic and distributed widely. Land animals include the large herds of caribou or reindeer that perhaps number as many as 5,000,000 to 25,000,000 head. There are also musk oxen, mountain sheep, wolves, foxes, and grizzly bears.

Among the birds found in the Arctic are the eider duck, the goose, the swan, the tern, and the gull. Salmon, cod, flounder, trout and halibut, and, of course, the seal, walrus, and whale live there, too.

## CAN AN ECHO TRAVEL THROUGH WATER?

Sound travels outward from its source at a speed of about 1,100 feet per second in the open air. Sound travels in waves much like the ripples made by a pebble thrown into the water. However, sound waves go out in all directions like the light from an electric bulb.

A sound wave may meet an obstacle and bounce back, or be reflected just as light is reflected. When a sound wave is thus reflected, it is heard as an echo. Therefore, an echo is sound repeated by reflection.

Not all obstacles can cause echoes; there are some objects which absorb the sound instead of reflecting it. If a sound is reflected by some obstacle, only one echo is heard. This is called a simple echo. If the sound is reflected by two or more obstacles, the echo may be repeated many times. The echo, however, becomes fainter each time until it dies away altogether. When repeated more than once, it is known as a compound echo, or reverberation.

An echo cannot be heard as a separate sound unless the sound is made some distance away from the reflecting surface. This allows enough time between sound and echo. At a distance of 550 feet from a wall, for example, the echo returns in just one second.

Whether an echo can travel through water depends on whether sound can travel through water—and we know that it can. In fact, sound travels through water at a speed of more than 4,700 feet per second! This ability of sound to produce an echo through water has proven very useful.

Ships are often equipped with devices for sending and receiving sound signals under water. By sending out sharp signals and timing the echoes, a navigator can measure the distance from his vessel to the ocean bottom or to any nearby vessel or obstacle!

# CHAPTER 2
# HOW OTHER CREATURES LIVE

Do you like to read detective stories or watch them on TV? What makes them exciting for you and me is the suspense. We want to find out who did it, or how, or why. But the world around us is full of mysteries, too.

## WHAT IS BIOLOGY?

Why do animals behave as they do? What makes plants grow in special ways? How does our body do this or that?

Man has always wanted to solve these mysteries of life. And just the way a detective proceeds on a case, the first thing that had to be done was to gather all the facts. The gathering and the study of these facts was called natural history.

Today we call this science biology. The word comes from two Greek words: *bios,* meaning "life," and *logos,* meaning "a study." So biology is the study of all organisms, plant and animal. What is studied about them is their form, their activities, their functions, and their environment.

But today our biologist-detectives are not satisfied just to collect a lot of facts, helter-skelter. They try to establish some links between the facts, some relationship. For example, they are interested in discovering the relationships that exist between man and the millions of living things that surround him. They want to know what effect these living things have had on man's own development.

Biologists are interested in the greatest mystery of all: how life first started on earth and why it took the forms it did. So they also study all the conditions that are necessary to life. And just as a detective bureau keeps a file, they try to classify every organism which exists on our planet.

In looking for clues that will answer their questions, biologists get a helping hand from nature. They dredge the icy depths of the oceans and scale the peaks of the tallest mountains looking for clues. They hack their way through steaming jungles, and peer for hours into microscopes. Sometimes they perform strange experiments in order to get at the mystery of life.

Biology is a very complex science. It has two main divisions: botany, which deals with plants; and zoology, which deals with animals. And each of these divisions is separated into dozens of subdivisions!

As we move about from place to place, we may feel changes in the temperature around us, but we don't expect the temperature of our body itself to change. And it doesn't. We are classified as "homeothermic,"

## WHAT IS THE BODY TEMPERATURE OF ANIMALS?

and in our class are included all warm-blooded animals, all mammals, domestic animals, and birds.

But there are animals whose body temperature does change with the temperature around them. They are called "poikilothermic," and they include insects, snakes, lizards, tortoises, frogs, and fishes. Their temperature tends to be slightly lower than the temperature of their environment. They are cold-blooded animals.

We know that the normal body temperature of man is considered

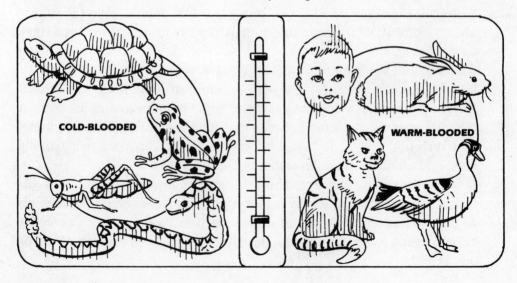

COLD-BLOODED

WARM-BLOODED

to be 98.6 degrees Fahrenheit. But there are many changes in the temperature that occur quite "normally." For example, man's body temperature is lowest about 4:00 A.M.; the skin temperature is lower than the internal temperature; taking in food raises the temperature for an hour or two; muscular work may raise the temperature; alcohol lowers the internal temperature.

The body temperature of animals has quite a range, going from 96 degrees in the elephant to 109 degrees in small birds. Here is how animals may be classified according to their body temperature:

From 96 to 101 degrees — man, monkey, mule, ass, horse, rat, mouse and elephant. From 100 to 103 degrees — cattle, sheep, dog, cat, rabbit, and pig. From 104 to 106 degrees — turkey, goose, duck, owl, pelican, and vulture. From 107 to 109 degrees — fowl, pigeon, and several small common birds.

Animals, like man, have to eliminate excess body heat in order to maintain a constant body temperature. Animals who don't sweat have to do this by panting — which is why your dog often pants on a hot day.

---

When we use the word "mammoth" today, we mean something that is huge or colossal. But there actually was an animal that lived long ago that is called the "mammoth." It was a kind of elephant that is now

## WHAT WAS THE MAMMOTH?

extinct and that lived in many different parts of the world during the Stone Age.

Even though this ancient type of elephant is called the "mammoth," it was about the same size as the Indian elephant that exists today. It had a kind of pointed skull and very unusual tusks curved in a spiral with the tips pointing to each other.

What made this elephant unique and quite different from the elephants we know today is that it was covered with long hair. In fact, the hair was so long that it almost reached the ground. The body was shaped into a great hump at the back of the neck, and the ears were small.

The whole body of this creature was covered with an undercoat of yellowish-brown wooly hair, and the long, black thicker hairs came out through this undercoat. The hair also grew on the ears. The first thing you'd probably say if you saw a mammoth today would be: "Get a haircut!"

Obviously an animal with so much hair on it would be more comfortable in a cold climate. And the mammoth is the only kind of elephant ever to exist that felt at home in a cold or Arctic climate. So it lived in Siberia quite comfortably, and probably survived there until a fairly recent period.

In other parts of the world, such as France and England, it survived only as long as the glacial period, or ice age, lasted. In fact, when things warmed up in England between glacial periods, the mammoth moved up north, following the retreating ice.

There were also mammoths in North America during that age, and some of these reached a height of 14 feet. Mammoths, because of their great weight, often sank into ice-cold mud which later became frozen. That's why frozen mammoths are still sometimes found very well preserved in places like Siberia.

---

When European explorers visited the New World, they often brought back with them whatever they considered strange and new. Thus the South American opossum was brought back from Brazil in 1500, and

## WHAT ARE MARSUPIALS?

Captain Cook in 1770 told about seeing kangaroos in Australia. Nobody in Europe had ever known about such creatures before — they were marsupials.

The marsupials are a separate order of animals. The name comes from the Greek word *marsupion,* which means "pouch." What sets these animals apart is that their young, after they are born, live and are fed in a pouch on their mother's body.

This is necessary because young marsupials are so tiny and helpless when they are born that they cannot take care of themselves. They do not even know how to eat. Even after they have grown to a fair size, young kangaroos and opossums run back to hide in their mother's pouch when they are frightened.

Judging from the fossils found in rocks, marsupials were once common in all parts of the world. Today almost all of them are found in Australia and the nearby islands. The only other true marsupials are the various species of opossums which live in North and South America.

Australian marsupials range in size from tiny molelike creatures only a few inches long to the giant kangaroos. Some of them, such as the bandicoots, look like rabbits. Others, such as the wombats, look like beavers. Still others, such as the thylacines and the Tasmanian wolves, look like wolves.

They may live on the ground or dwell in the trees like monkeys. Some of the phalangers, which are one family of marsupials, can even glide from tree to tree like flying squirrels. The food of marsupials is quite varied. Some eat only vegetables, others are meat-eaters or insect-eaters, and some eat anything they can find.

---

A bloodhound, of course, is a breed of dog. But how did it develop? Where did it come from?

The history of the dog itself goes back many hundreds of thousands

## WHAT IS A BLOODHOUND?

of years. Some scientists believe that dogs are the result of the mating of their cousins, the wolves and the jackals. It is generally believed however that our modern dogs and the wolves are descended from a very remote common ancestor.

During the many years that dogs have been tamed, men have developed more than 200 breeds of dogs. Sometimes they have bred dogs for strength, like that of the mastiff; for speed, like the greyhound; or for keenness of scent, like that of the bloodhound.

The bloodhound is typical of the breed of dog known as the hound. It is probably a descendant of the dog which at one time was called the "St. Hubert." Hounds generally have smooth coats, are heavy, and have drooping ears and upper lips.

Like all hounds, the bloodhounds follow the quarry by scent—keener in them than in any other dog. They are slow put persistent, and if they lose the scent they cast back until they find the trail again. It is these two qualities, their keen scent and their ability to be persistent, that make bloodhounds ideal for tracking down escaped criminals and for other use by police.

There are many other interesting types of hounds. For example, otter hounds, harriers, beagles, and bassets are all smaller than bloodhounds and are used in hunting small game, such as rabbits.

The pointer is a hound that is one of the best bird dogs. It was given its name because it "points" at the game.

Deer live in all parts of the world except Australia, New Zealand, Madagascar, and Southern Africa. There are about 50 different species of deer, but they all have certain things in common.

## WHY DO DEER SHED THEIR ANTLERS?

Deer are vegetarians who feed on moss, bark, buds, leaves, or water plants. They are usually very timid animals, and they depend on their speed for safety. They generally feed at night. They have very good eyesight, and their senses of hearing and smell are so sharp that they are able to detect danger easily. Deer vary in size from the little pudu, which is only a foot tall, to the great moose, which may weigh more than 1,000 pounds!

The chief distinguishing marks of the deer are the antlers. Nearly all the males have antlers, and in the case of the caribou and reindeer, females have them too. The antlers are not hollow, like the horns of cattle, but are made of a honeycomb structure. Each spring, the male deer grows a new pair of antlers, and each winter he loses them after the mating season is over. In some varieties of deer, the antlers are single shafts, in others there may be as many as 11 branches to each antler! Since the number of branches varies with age, you can tell how old a deer is from its antlers.

The first year, two knoblike projections appear on the deer's forehead. These are called the "pedicles," and they are never lost. The antlers break off from the pedicle each spring and new antlers are grown during the summer. The second year, a straight shaft grows out of the

pedicle, and in the third year, the first branch appears.

When the antlers are growing, they are covered with a sensitive skin called the "velvet." This is filled with blood vessels which feed the antlers and build up the bone. When the antlers have reached their full size, after a period of two to four months, the blood supply is cut off from the velvet by the formation of a ring around the base of the antlers. This makes the velvet wither and dry up, and it finally falls off. Usually, the deer help by rubbing their antlers against trees.

---

One of the gentlest of all animals is the hare. When you consider how mild, timid, and defenseless this creature is, you might wonder how it can survive in a world full of enemies. But then you've also probably

# WHAT IS THE DIFFERENCE BETWEEN RABBITS AND HARES?

noticed its strong hindlegs. Those legs give it plenty of speed and endurance. And, of course, you know how rapidly hares and rabbits breed. That's another reason why they manage to survive.

Hares and rabbits are rodents, which means they have long, sharp front teeth. Their hindlegs are longer than their forelegs, so that they actually run faster uphill than downhill! When they are pursued, they resort to some clever tricks. One is to crisscross their tracks, and the other is to take huge leaps in order to break the scent. They can also signal danger to each other by thumping the ground with their hindfeet.

Hares and rabbits are purely vegetarians, but they can live very well on the inner bark of trees. There are many differences between hares and rabbits. Hares are larger, and their feet and ears are longer. Hares do not dig burrows or live in groups, as do rabbits. Hares are born open-eyed and furry, while rabbits are born blind and hairless. Hares and rabbits never mate.

North America is the home of many different types of hares. One of the best known is the jack hare, which is usually mistakenly called "jack rabbit." It is found throughout the West. Jack hares are more than two feet in length and have enormous ears. Jacks are so fast that they can sometimes make a leap of 20 feet. They are a geat nuisance to farmers in the West, and are often rounded up and killed by thousands.

The March hare, whom we know from "Alice in Wonderland," is a common European hare. In March, its mating season, it disregards caution, coming out at all times of the day and performing amusing acrobatic feats.

Rabbits came originally from the western shores of the Mediterranean. They are social animals, living together in burrows, called "warrens." A rabbit may mate when it is six months old. Its young are born within a month. There may be from three to eight in a litter and a female rabbit may bear from four to eight litters in a year. So if the rabbit has no natural enemies, it can become quite a nuisance. In Australia for instance, three pairs of rabbits were introduced many years ago, and today the rabbit is a great national pest!

---

One of the most interesting animals to be found anywhere is the mole. Moles live in every part of the United States and there are about 30 different species. But they are so seldom seen by people that they have

## CAN A MOLE SEE?

become a kind of mysterious creature.

You can find a mole by looking for the long ridges of cracked earth it makes across fields. This is the roof of its tunnel, for the mole spends its whole life in darkness under the ground.

A mole grows to about six inches in size. It has a fine, velvety fur, the color of a mouse, and a pink tail about an inch long. It has no neck at all, and its ears are tiny openings hidden in the fur. A mole does have eyes, but they are tiny points covered with fur and skin. This is why it was once believed that moles are blind. A mole can see, but very poorly.

If you picked up a mole and put it down on the ground, it would race about until it found a soft spot and would begin to dig at once. A mole is one of the most efficient diggers in nature. Its forefeet are powerful and shaped like spades. It can dig a burrow and disappear into it in less than one minute! In a single night, it can dig a tunnel 225 feet long.

Moles usually live in a colony in a sort of fortress undergound. From the surface, we see a little hillock of earth called a "molehill." Right under it, there are two circular galleries or passageways, one above the other. Vertical passageways connect them, so the mole can move up and down. The upper gallery has five of these openings which go down to a central chamber where the mole rests.

A whole series of complicated tunnels lead from these galleries and from the central chamber to the feeding grounds, to the nest, and even to an "emergency" exit. These underground tunnels are so well built that field mice and gophers often use them to get roots and plants for food. But it isn't too safe for other animals to venture into a mole's home. It has such sharp front teeth that it can fight viciously and kill mice much bigger than itself. Its chief food, however, consists of insects and earthworms. A mole is so greedy that if it is unable to get food for 12 hours it will die!

The porcupine has always been considered an annoying, disagreeable animal. In fact, even Shakespeare described it that way. In Hamlet, there is the line: "Like quills upon the fretful porcupine."

## DO PORCUPINES SHOOT THEIR QUILLS?

Actually, the porcupine is quite a harmless animal, who simply likes to be let alone. During the winter, it curls up in a hollow log or cave and sleeps most of the time. In the summer, it moves slowly through the woods in search of bark, twigs, roots, and leaves of trees and shrubs.

Porcupines can be found in Europe, Africa, India, and South America as well as in our own country and Canada. The American species of porcupine is about three feet long and weighs from 15 to 30 pounds. Its quills are about seven inches long and are yellowish-white, with black tips. The quills grow among the softer hairs of the porcupine, and consist of a shaft with a hard point.

When the porcupine is born, the quills are fine and silky. It takes them several weeks to thicken into hard quills. When a porcupine is attacked, it bristles up its coat of quills and curls into a bristling ball.

These quills are fastened rather loosely into the body of the porcupine. Since the porcupine will sometimes swing its tail into the face of an enemy, the quills come out easily during such an action. This is what has made people think a porcupine "shoots" its quills. It doesn't. They just fly out.

The porcupine usually sleeps during the day and comes out to feed at night. It uses its long, sharp claws to climb trees, and then it sits on a limb to gnaw away at the bark and twigs. It crams bark, twigs, leaves, all into its mouth at once. Because of its liking for bark, the porcupine does much damage to forests. A single porcupine has been known to kill 100 trees in a winter!

Another strong liking the porcupine has is for salt. It will walk boldly into camps and gnaw any article that has been touched by salt or even by perspiring hands!

Some people believe that raccoons wash all their food before eating it. There is some truth to this. Most raccoons do wash their food, and there have been cases where raccoons refused to eat food when they couldn't find any water nearby!

# DO RACCOONS WASH THEIR FOOD?

But on the other hand, raccoons have been known to eat food even when they were some distance from water, though perhaps they weren't too happy about it. And some raccoons have been observed to eat without ever washing their food.

Nobody really knows why raccoons wash their food. It isn't because of cleanliness, since they may wash it in water that is actually dirtier than the food! Besides, they will wash food caught in the water, which certainly doesn't need washing. So the reason is probably that the raccoon enjoys feeling the food in water. It seems to make it tastier!

The name "raccoon" comes from the Algonquin Indian word *arakhumen*. The raccoon lives from southern Canada to Panama, except in the high Rockies. Raccoons vary in size from 25 to 35 inches in length. In weight they range from three to twenty-five pounds. The general color of the long fur is grayish or brownish. The 10-inch tail is dark brown with four to six yellowish rings. The eyes are covered with a black mask. The ears are medium-sized, the nose pointed, and the front feet are used like hands.

Raccoons live in places where there is water and trees for dens. Their food, which they hunt at night, is principally crayfish, clams, fish and frogs, which they catch in the muddy water. In season raccoons also feed on nuts, berries, fruit, and paticularly young corn.

The year-round home, or den, where the young are born is usually in the hollow limb or trunk of a tree. Raccoons give birth to young but once a year, with four or five to a litter. By fall, the young raccoons are large enough to start their life alone.

Do you know what the word "armadillo" means? It's a Spanish word meaning "the little armored one." And that's just what an armadillo is, a little mammal with a bony covering that is like armor.

## WHAT IS AN ARMADILLO?

There are ten different kinds of armadillos living from southern United States to southern South America. The upper parts of armadillos are covered with bony shells. These include one on the head and two solid pieces on the back. These two pieces are connected by a flexible center section made up of movable bands. This enables the armadillo to twist and turn.

The number of these bands in the center is sometimes used as a name for the armadillo. For example, there is the seven-banded the eight-banded, and the nine-banded armadillo. The nine-banded armadillo is the only one found in the United States. The tail of the armadillo is also completely covered by armor—except in the case of one kind, and naturally it's called the soft-tailed armadillo!

A very curious thing about the armadillo is that its teeth are simple pegs without enamel. It's one of those contradictions that nature seems fond of. A shell of armor on the body—and soft teeth! Most of the animals have just one set of teeth they are born with, and that's all.

As a result of having such teeth, the armadillo has to eat soft food such as ants, termites, larvae, grubs, and bugs. As you know, such food is found in leaves and the soft ground, so to get at it the armadillo has to dig for it. Nature made up for the soft teeth by

giving the armadillo long, strong claws and powerful forearms. An armadillo can dig faster than a dog! And it uses the claws and fore-arms to dig its burrow or to make itself a hole quickly into which it can escape from its enemies.

The way most armadillos escape from their enemies is by digging or running away. Only one kind, the three-banded armadillo, rolls itself into a ball. Its shell is much heavier than that of the others, so this becomes a good way of protecting itself.

---

**WHERE DID ELEPHANTS ORIGINATE?**

Thousands of years ago, many kinds of giant monsters roamed about the great forests then covering the earth. Even though these beasts were immense in size, they were not able to endure the hardships they had to undergo, brought about by changing climate and disappearance of food.

One by one they perished, until of all those huge animals, there are only two species remaining, the African and Asiatic elephants. The ancestors of the elephant were great monsters, known as "mammoths." Their skeletons can be seen in museums, and they are quite awesome sights! Their bones have been dug up in caves and river beds in North America and Europe. In far-off Siberia, the carcass of one was found frozen hard in ice, per-fectly preserved even to its eyes!

Although elephants seem to have once inhabited many parts of the earth, they are now found in their wild state only in Africa and tropical Asia.

Elephants are the largest land animals, and in many ways, among the most interesting. They are mild and gentle, and quite intelligent. They are more easily trained than any other beast except the domestic dog.

The shape of the elephant's legs, like four huge pillars, is necessary to support its immense weight. Its ivory tusks are really overgrown teeth. These tusks are used to dig up roots for food and also as weapons for defense. The brain of the elephant is comparatively small, consid-ering the size of the animal.

The most remarkable part of the elephant's body is its trunk. It is an extension of the nose and upper lip, and it serves the elephant as hand, arm, nose, and lips, all in one. There are about 40,000 muscles in the trunk, so it is very strong and flexible. The tip of the trunk ends in a sort of finger which is so sensitive that it can pick up a small pin!

There are few animals that have played as important a role in history as the horse. This is because the horse has been so useful in warfare. Can you imagine what wandering tribes, invading armies, knights,

## WHO FIRST TAMED THE HORSE?

and soldiers all over the world would have done without the horse during the last few thousand years?

We can trace the ancestors of the horse back millions of years. But who first tamed the horse, the animal that we know? It is impossible to say. We know that prehistoric man used the horse as one of his chief sources of food. This was probably long before he thought of using the horse for riding.

The earliest pictures and carvings of horses were made by European cave men about 15,000 years ago. The horse in these pictures is very much like today's Mongolian pony. In these pictures and carvings there are marks that suggest a bridle, so perhaps the horse was already tamed!

It is probable however, that the wandering tribes in central Asia were the first to tame the horse, and from there the horse came to Europe and Asia Minor. We know there were horses in Babylonia as long ago as 3,000 B.C.

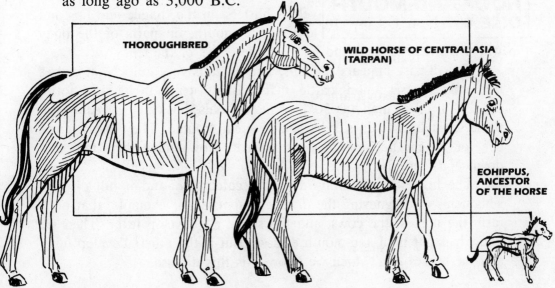

THOROUGHBRED

WILD HORSE OF CENTRAL ASIA (TARPAN)

EOHIPPUS, ANCESTOR OF THE HORSE

Because the horse was tamed before historic records began, it is very difficult to trace the origin of any of the modern breeds. The oldest and purest breed of saddle horse is the Arabian. They have been bred for at least fifteen centuries! They are small horses, their legs are slender, and their feet are small. Their backs are short and strong.

When Julius Caesar invaded England he found horses there. In his time, they were probably small, hardy animals. Later on, during the days of the knights, horses were bred chiefly for size and strength, and used as war horses. Then when gunpowder was invented, speed became more important than strength or size, so faster horses were bred.

As horse racing became more widespread, horses from the Arabs, Turks, and Persians were brought into England. Our modern thorough-bred horse is descended from these combinations.

A thoroughbred, by the way, is any horse eligible to be registered in the General Stud Book. It was begun in England in 1791 and traces the pedigree of horses, going back to about 1690!

---

If you live on a farm or have anything to do with cattle, then you've probably heard people talk about this disease, also called foot-and-mouth disease. It is a highly contagious disease that affects practically all cloven-footed animals.

## WHAT IS HOOF-AND-MOUTH DISEASE?

When an animal gets this disease, it develops blisters on the tongue and lips and around the mouth, on parts of the body where the skin is thin, and between the claws of the feet.

The disease appears suddenly and spreads very quickly. It causes tremendous losses among cattle. If the disease strikes in a serious form, it may kill off as many as 50% of the animals that catch it! And even those animals that do survive are in great trouble. They lose a great deal of weight because they cannot eat. Cows have their milk cut down considerably.

The horse, by the way, does not catch hoof-and-mouth disease. This helps in diagnosing the disease. Suppose, for example, that on a farm the horses, the cows, and the swine all develop fever. Then we know it is not hoof-and-mouth disease. But if the others develop fever and the horses don't, then we know it is this disease.

This disease is caused by a virus that presents quite a problem. For one thing, it is the smallest virus known. The virus that causes smallpox, just to give you an idea, is 10,000 times larger! Another problem is that this virus can resist being destroyed if the conditions are right. It can remain active in hay for 30 days. It can remain active for 76 days at freezing temperature! And it can resist a great many antiseptics.

Still another complication is that there are six types of virus that cause hoof-and-mouth disease. So if an animal develops an immunity to one of these viruses, it may still get the disease from any of the other five!

---

Because we have all seen trained seals in the circus, and because seals are such fun to watch in the zoo, they have a kind of fascination for us. Yet surprisingly little is known by most people about these creatures.

## CAN SEALS LIVE UNDER WATER?

The order of seals includes the fur seals, the sea lions, hair seals, sea elephants, and the walrus. Seals are mammals, and they stand halfway between typical mammals such as cows and dogs, and such sea mammals as whales.

Actually, seals are descended from land mammals, which means that at one time they had to adapt themselves to living in the water. They have not lived in the water for as long as whales have. The result is that seals are not nearly so well adapted to aquatic life as whales are.

Seals cannot live under water all the time. Not only that, but their young must be born on land. In most cases, the babies must be taught to swim by their mothers! So you can see why a seal is halfway between a land mammal and a sea mammal.

As they adapted themselves for life in the water, certain changes took place. They developed webbed hind-limbs and paddlelike fore-limbs to be able to swim fast. They acquired a layer of blubber to keep them warm. They have also either lost or reduced the size of their external, or outside, ears in order to lessen water resistance. And they began to feed on such sea creatures as squid, octopuses, and fish.

Although nature has changed the seal greatly for water life, seals spend a good deal of time on land. They like to sun themselves or sleep on beaches or ice floes. On shore, they move either by wriggling along or by dragging themselves with their fore-flippers.

In the United States, the most familiar seals are the California sea lions. They are active and intelligent. They can be trained easily to do tricks, such as juggling and balancing balls on the ends of their noses.

The habits of seals make them an easy prey for man. This is especially so during their breeding season when they can be approached on the beaches or ice floes. For centuries, the Eskimos have used seals for food, clothing, and their oil for cooking and light.

---

It is hard to believe that the porpoise is not a fish, but a mammal. Yet it is just as much a mammal as the cow in the fields. Porpoises, dolphins and whales form the order called "Cetacea" of the group of aquatic mammals.

## IS THE PORPOISE A MAMMAL?

Actually, dolphins belong to the whale family and porpoises are a variety of dolphins. All these animals may be given the general name of whales, or cetaceans.

There are a great many differences between porpoises and other whales and fish. The baby porpoise is fed on its mother's milk like other little mammals. It is not hatched from an egg, but is born alive. Porpoises have no gills and breathe air through their lungs. Internally, porpoises have a skeleton, circulatory system, brain, and vital organs that are quite unlike those of fish.

Another important difference is the existence of blubber. Mammals are warm-blooded animals, and blubber conserves their animal heat in the cold waters.

The common porpoise is about 5½ feet long. The head is rounded in front, and the underjaw projects slightly. It has a wide mouth with between 80 and 100 teeth. A porpoise is black or grey in color above, and white below, with black flippers.

The porpoise prefers to live in waters near the coast rather than the open sea. It inhabits the North Atlantic but is quite rare in the Mediterranean. Porpoises live in great herds and seem to delight in following ships. There are some species of porpoises that appear in the South Atlantic and the Pacific Oceans.

Porpoise oil, which is obtained from the soft fat of the head and jaw, is used as a lubricant in the manufacture of watches and other delicate instruments because it doesn't gum up and can resist very low temperatures.

---

When the average person thinks of a reptile, he thinks of a snake. But actually, this class of animals includes many other creeping and crawling creatures.

## WHAT IS A REPTILE?

In the animal kingdom, reptiles rank between the amphibians and the birds. Amphibians are animals that can live both on land and in the water. As a matter of fact, scientists believe that birds developed from the reptiles several million years ago. At that time, the reptiles were the the ruling class among animals, and they were often of giant size. But these giant reptiles died out, and the reptiles that are living today are comparatively small. The largest of these are crocodiles and the python snakes.

In many ways, reptiles are much like amphibians. All are cold-blooded, creeping animals with backbones. They are distinguished mainly by their lungs and their skin. Amphibians breathe through gills when they are young, and later many kinds develop lungs. Reptiles, on the other hand, breathe by means of lungs all their lives.

The skin of amphibians is smooth and clammy, being kept moist

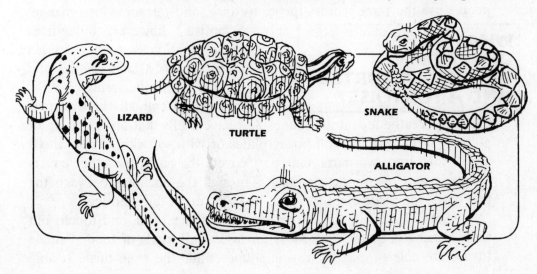

LIZARD

TURTLE

SNAKE

ALLIGATOR

by special slime glands. Water passes easily through this skin; therefore, most amphibians dry out and die if kept out of water for long. Reptiles have no slime glands, and their skin is dry and scaly. Because water cannot pass out through their skin, reptiles are able to live entirely on land.

The reptiles living today are divided into four main groups: the turtles, the crocodilians, the lizards, and snakes, and the strange lizard-like tuatara of New Zealand.

Turtles and tortoises differ from other reptiles in having their bodies surrounded by a bony shell covered with horny shields. All turtles and tortoises lay eggs. Many of the turtles live in or near bodies of fresh water, while tortoises live entirely upon land.

The alligators and crocodiles and their relatives are long, four-limbed animals having scales or plates covering their bodies. Alligators and crocodiles are so much alike that it may take an expert to tell them apart. In the United States, however, the alligators have a shorter and broader snout than the crocodiles.

Lizards and snakes belong to the highest order of reptiles. The main difference between lizards and snakes is in the structure of the jaws. In snakes, both upper and lower jaws have movable halves with sharp recurved teeth.

---

Turtles, tortoises, and terrapins all belong to a group of four-legged reptiles that have hard outer shells, scaly skins, and horny beaks. Most people use the three words—turtle, tortoise, and terrapin—interchange-

## WHAT IS THE DIFFERENCE BETWEEN A TURTLE AND A TORTOISE?

ably. Scientists, however, sometimes make this distinction: a turtle is a sea reptile; a tortoise is a land reptile; and a terrapin is a fresh-water reptile.

It is correct to call all three turtles. They all breathe air through lungs and have shells that are made up of a "bony box" covered with horny plates or with soft skin. These shells are divided into two parts. One part covers the back; the other covers the underpart of the turtle's body. Through the openings between the two parts, the turtle can thrust out its head, neck, tail, and legs.

Turtles have well-developed senses of sight, taste, and touch, but their hearing is quite poor. Most turtles eat all kinds of food. Female turtles are able to make a hissing sound, while the male turtle is able to give a kind of "grunt." Some of the giant land turtles are even able to bellow!

The largest of living turtles is the leatherback, which is a sea turtle. It usually weighs about 1,000 pounds, and the biggest specimen on record is over 8 feet long and weighs 1,500 pounds!

Turtle soup is made from the flesh of the green turtle, which is also a sea turtle. It is usually found in tropical seas, and may weigh as much as 500 pounds. Tortoise shell, which is quite expensive, is obtained from the hawksbill turtle. It is the smallest of the sea turtles and is rarely more than 3 feet long. Its horny shell consists of separate, clear, horny shields of dark brown, richly marbled with yellow.

The biggest North American turtle is the alligator snapping turtle. It weighs up to 150 pounds and lives in the Mississippi region. Snappers, which are fresh-water turtles, have long, large tails and very strong, sharp jaws.

The most common North American land turtle is the wood, which has brick-red skin. It can become quite a friendly pet and will learn to take food from one's fingers. Turtles hibernate during the winter months, hiding either in the bottom of ponds or in holes in the ground. Turtles sometimes live for 200 years or more!

---

In order for there to be a "queen bee," there must be a colony of bees. But not all bees live in colonies. There are species of bees called "solitary" bees. Among them there are only two kinds of bees, the males and the egg-laying females.

## WHAT MAKES A QUEEN BEE A "QUEEN"?

But bees that live in colonies, called "social bees," have a third form of bee known as "workers." The workers are really female bees that ordinarily don't lay eggs. So in a colony of social bees we have the workers, the males, who are called "drones," and the one egg-laying female, the mother of the colony, who is called the "queen."

Here is how a queen bumblebee spends her life. She passes the winter in a hole dug in a sandbank or other suitable place. She is the only member of the colony that lives through the winter! In the spring, she starts a new colony.

She first looks for a home, perhaps a deserted mouse nest. She heaps the soft material of the nest together and hollows out a place under it to serve as a nursery. Then she visits flowers for pollen and nectar and places a lump of beebread in the dry hollow she has prepared. She lays some eggs on this lump, covers them with wax, and sits over them, keeping the cold air away with her body.

Near her she has made a large waxen cell, called a "honeypot," which she has filled with enough honey for food to last until her eggs hatch. As soon as her first brood of young have grown big enough to use their wings, they take over most of mother's work. They prepare wax, make the beebread, and keep the honeypot filled to use in bad weather.

During the early part of the season, the only bees born are the workers. But before the summer is over, young queens and males, or drones, will also grow up in the colony. In the fall, the colony breaks up. All that the queen bee has done all summer long is lay eggs!

Among the honeybees, the queen lays all the eggs, but she cannot care for them. She may lay more than 1,500 eggs per day and about 250,000 in a season! She lays fertilized eggs that develop into workers or queens, depending on the needs of the colony. The unfertilized eggs develop into drones.

Young queens are reared in special queen cells. Before they emerge, the mother queen and about half the workers swarm off to start the new colony. The first young queen to emerge kills her sister queens in their cells and thus becomes the new mother queen!

---

In the United States alone, termites do about $40,000,000 worth of damage a year! Strangely enough, these creatures which are such a problem to man today, have existed for millions of years. Primitive termites probably lived during the age

## WHAT ARE TERMITES?

of dinosaurs!

Today, they are found in every state in the United States and in southern Canada. The greatest number are to be found in the rainy tropical regions around the world. There are more than 2,000 kinds of termites, about 50 of which are found in the United States.

Termites are insects that look like ants, but which are quite different from them. They have thick waists, a light color, and evenly curved feelers, or antennae.

Termites live in colonies in wood. They cut out the wood and form rooms for the colony. A colony of termites will consist of a king and

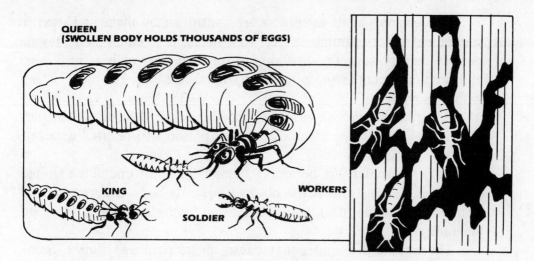

**QUEEN
(SWOLLEN BODY HOLDS THOUSANDS OF EGGS)**

**KING**

**SOLDIER**

**WORKERS**

queen, soldiers, and workers. The soldiers protect the colony from its enemies. They do not have wings and are blind, but they are the fighters.

The job of the workers is to feed the colony. They eat the wood and then feed this digested wood to all the other termites. In the hind intestine of a worker is a liquid. When this liquid is looked at through a microscope, thousands of single-celled animals, or protozoans, are seen. The protozoans turn the celluose of the wood into sugar. The sugar is digested by the worker and fed to the others.

Wood can be so treated that termites will not attack it. One method is to soak it with coal tar creosote under pressure, so that the creosote reaches the center. When building a house, care should be taken not to let any untreated wood come closer than two feet from the ground. Although moist soil is necessary for the life of most termites, there are dry-wood termites in the South that can live without such soil.

There is hardly a place in the world you can go where you won't find spiders. They can be found at sea level and on Mt. Everest, in forests, meadows, swamps, deserts, and in caves underground.

## WHICH SPIDERS ARE POISONOUS?

Many people have a fear of spiders, because some types are known to be poisonous. All spiders, except two species, have poison glands. But this doesn't mean that the spiders with poison glands can harm man.

The poison glands in spiders are controlled by them and used in special ways. For example, spiders who spin nets to catch their prey do not use their poison. Those who hunt for their prey or hide in flowers and capture insects by grasping them with their fangs, kill their victims with poison.

All spiders, however, use their poison in self defense. When they are trapped and escape is impossible, the poison will be used as a last resort.

Very few spiders are poisonous to man. The only one in the United States that is dangerous is the black widow. Its body is about half an inch long and shiny black, and it has a red hour-glass shaped mark on the underside.

The bite of this spider may cause severe pain and illness. Some spiders whose bite is poisonous to man live in Australia. The large so-called "deadly" tarantulas and banana spiders have never actually killed any person. They may cause one's arm or whatever is bitten to swell greatly and to ache for a few days.

The majority of spiders are no more dangerous to man than wasps or hornets. In fact, a great many spiders won't bite even if you hold them in your hand. So unless you know the spider is a black widow, you can feel pretty safe with one.

The most amazing thing about spiders of course, is their ability to spin webs. The silk of spiders is manufactured in certain of their abdominal glands. The silk is forced through many tiny holes from the spinning organs at the tip of the abdomen. It comes out as a liquid which becomes solid on contact with the air.

There are many kinds of silk, depending on the type of spider, and there is a great variety of webs, including one built underwater!

---

When the presence of the boll weevil within the United States was first discovered, cotton growers refused to believe that this little brown beetle could cause serious damage. The discovery was made about

## WHAT IS A BOLL WEEVIL?

1892, in southern Texas. About 30 years later, it was estimated that the boll weevil had decreased the annual cotton crop by more than 6,000,000 bales!

The boll weevil is a native of Central America. It worked northward through Mexico, and crossed the border into Texas at Brownsville. Like most insects, it has a keen sense of smell. Experiments have shown that the boll weevils which have just come forth in the final, or beetle stage of their development can head straight for a cotton field several miles away!

When full-grown, the beetle is about a quarter of an inch long. Its jaws are at the tip of a snout well arranged for boring holes in cotton buds. The beetle sleeps all winter under dry grass and leaves, or in cracks in the ground. In the spring, when the cotton buds are starting to form, it begins its destructive work.

The female insect bores into the buds and lays her eggs in them. Within three or four days, the eggs hatch, and the small grubs feed on the inside of the bud.

The young "squares," as the flower buds are called, are the favorite breeding places; but when squares can no longer be found, the beetles attack the cotton bolls or fiber-filled pods. The worms remain inside the bolls during the period when they are changing into beetles.

There are four or five generations of weevils during a season, so it is easy to understand what a large amount of damage they can cause. The infested buds usually drop off without maturing, and the cotton fibers of infested bolls are useless.

---

One of the most fascinating and remarkable creatures in the world is the ant. There are more than 3,500 different kinds of ants, and they are found almost everywhere in the world.

## WHAT ARE ARMY ANTS?

All ants are very much alike except in size. Ants may be as small as $\frac{1}{16}$ of an inch, or as long as 2 inches. And all ants live in colonies. But there are tremendous differences in their way of life and their habits.

One of the most interesting types of ants, for example, is the "army ant." It eats living things! In Africa, there is a type of army ant called the "driver" ant. These ants go out in armies of many thousands. They kill and eat everything in their way.

Now you might wonder, "How can a little insect like the ant eat and kill everything in its way?" Well, there are thousands and thousands of them. Even the largest animals run away when they are coming. And if a creature cannot run—then good-bye! The army ants will kill and eat it, whether it is a fly or a crocodile or a wounded lion!

Army ants in the Americas eat only small things. They are called "legionary" ants. They may be found in the southern United States, and in Central and South America. Legionary ants travel in lines of thousands of individuals. In Mexico, people move out of their houses when they come. The ants eat all the roaches, rats, mice, and lizards that may be in the houses. Then the people move back to vermin-free houses!

Did you know that there are also ants who own slaves? These are the Amazon ants. The Amazon workers are all soldiers, and so they cannot gather food or tend to the young. So they must raid other ants to get slaves who will do this work.

They raid the nests of certain small, black ants. They kill any ants who try to resist them. Then they take the cocoons and larvae to their own homes. When the black ants come out of the cocoons, they will work in the Amazon colony, just like slaves!

---

Have you ever turned over a flat stone or a rotting log, and seen a little wormlike creature running quickly away from the light? The chances are it was a centipede.

## DOES A CENTIPEDE REALLY HAVE ONE HUNDRED FEET?

Of course you didn't actually have a chance to count all its feet to see if it really had a hundred of them! The name "centipede" means "100-footed," and some species of this creature actually have 100 feet. Some, in fact, even have more legs than that! And some have only 30 legs.

While it seems rather amazing to us that any living thing can have so many feet, such creatures are not as rare in nature as we might think. There is a whole group of animals called "Myriapoda." This means "many-footed," and it includes not only the centipedes, but also the millepedes. Can you guess what "millepedes" means? You're right if you said 1,000-legged! So the centipede is not the champion when it comes to greatest number of legs. Incidentally, this type of creature is one of the oldest in existence. According to scientists, there have been

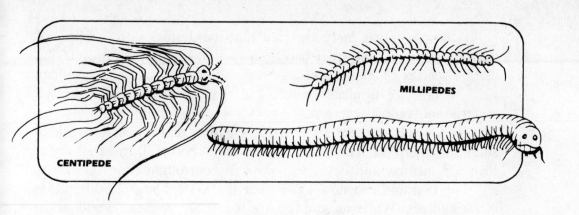

CENTIPEDE

MILLIPEDES

centipedes and millipedes for millions of years!

While some human beings have trouble not stumbling with just two feet—a centipede can manage his hundred or so feet quite easily. The legs are arranged in pairs, and each pair grows out of a segment of the centipede's body, which is flat and has many joints.

On the section next to the head of the centipede, there are two long feelers and two poison-bearing claws. The poison of most centipedes is harmless to man, but in the tropics there are certain species, 8 to 10 inches long, whose bite may be serious. In fact, such centipedes have been known to kill small birds!

Centipedes develop from eggs laid in the open. Some kinds are hatched with their full number of legs. Others start with seven pairs and add a new set each time they shed their skin, until they are full-grown. Centipedes come out at night to hunt their food, and during the day they hide under rocks or in dead wood.

Have you ever been out camping or walking in a beautiful country spot, when suddenly everything was spoiled by a swarm of mosquitoes? These little creatures cannot only ruin our pleasure, they can make

## DO ANY AMERICAN MOSQUITOES CARRY DISEASE?

us quite miserable with their stubborn attacks.

For a long time, man considered mosquitoes annoying and troublesome—but that was all. It wasn't until the end of the century that we began to discover they were dangerous, too.

A few scientists had suspected that mosquitoes were carriers of disease, but no actual proof had been found. Then it was proven that certain species of mosquitoes carry the worms which cause elephantiasis, a horrible tropical disease, and that other mosquitoes spread malaria and yellow fever.

As a result of these discoveries, scientists really went to work to study the mosquito. They have studied their species, learned all about their life history, and developed ways of controlling them.

For example, we now know that there are about 1,000 species of mosquitoes. While mosquitoes are found all over the world, some species are found everywhere and other species are found only in certain regions. In the United States, there are about 70 species of mosquitoes.

One of these is the Anopheles mosquito, and several species of this type in the United States are carriers of malaria. An Anopheles has black spots on its wings. It stands, when at rest, with its head down and its bill and body in a straight line.

There is another mosquito in the United States that is quite dangerous, and this is the Aedes mosquito. It carries yellow fever. This mosquito has white stripes around its legs and crosswise on its back. It rests with its bill at an angle to its body.

The best thing to do about mosquitoes is to eliminate them!

---

It's a natural thing to consider the housefly a nuisance. It makes an irritating buzzing sound; it annoys you when it crawls on your skin; and so on. For ages that's what man considered the fly to be—just a nuisance.

## WHY DO FLIES RUB THEIR LEGS TOGETHER?

It wasn't until the twentieth century that we found out that the innocent-looking housefly is one of man's worst enemies. It was discovered that these flies carried disease germs that cause the death of millions of people every year!

When you see a fly rubbing its legs together, it is just cleaning itself, and scraping off some of the material that has gathered there. But how dangerous that material may be! It may be the bacteria of such diseases as typhoid fever, tuberculosis, or dysentery. Flies get such germs from garbage and sewage. Then, if they happen to touch our food, the germs spread to the food, and if we eat it, we may become infected.

How does the fly carry these germs around? If you were to look at a fly under the magnifying glass, you would notice that the fly's body isn't smooth at all. Its whole body, its claws, and its padded feet, are covered with bristling hairs. The fly's tongue is also coated with sticky glue.

This means that practically any place the fly stops for even a moment, it's going to pick up things that stick to its body, its feet, or its tongue. In fact, each foot on its three pairs of legs has claws and two hairy pads—so it can make plenty of "pick-ups!" By the way, a sticky liquid is secreted by the fly's pads, and it is this which enables the fly to walk upside down on the ceiling, or any surface.

Did you know that flies are among the oldest insects known? Fossil remains of flies have been found that are millions of years old. Will we ever get rid of flies altogether? The only way we can bring this about is to prevent them from breeding. And for this to be done, conditions have to be made very sanitary all over the world!

---

In the Bible, we read of plagues of locusts descending upon a people and causing great suffering. Of course, in those times such a plague was considered a punishment from God, just as floods, droughts, and disease.

## WHAT CAUSES PLAGUES OF LOCUSTS?

But plagues of locusts have appeared in other times and in other lands, too. In the western United States, there was such a plague from 1874 to 1876 that did more than $200,000,000 worth of damage!

The word "locust" has been applied to many members of the grasshopper family. A locust is actually any of a group of insects that belong to a family called "Acrididae." The so-called 17-year locust is not really a locust but a cicada.

Many scientists have been studying the question of why these insects descend on a region in great swarms at certain times, and seem to disappear between those times.

It seems that the species of locust that produces the "plague" exists in two phases, or periods. The two phases are solitary and gregarious, or in groups. In these two extreme phases, the locusts are quite different. They differ in color, form, structure, and behavior.

In the solitary phase, the locusts do not congregate and are sluggish in behavior. Their color matches that of their surroundings. In the gregarious phase, the locusts have a black and yellow color, congregate in great groups, are very active and nervous, and they even have a higher temperature. There are other differences as well. The solitary phase is the normal phase for the locusts.

When, for some reason, crowding is forced on the locusts in the solitary phase, they produce locusts of the gregarious type. These locusts are restless and irritable; they begin to wander; they are joined by others; a great swarm develops, and soon millions of them are ready to descend on a region in the form of a plague!

---

The migration of birds has fascinated man since the very beginning of history. Did you know that Homer wrote about it in 1000 B.C.; it's mentioned in the Bible; and the great Greek philosopher, Aristotle,

## HOW DO BIRDS KNOW WHEN TO MIGRATE?

studied the question?

And yet, so many thousands of years later, we still don't have the complete answers to the fascinating phenomenon of the migration of birds. By this migration, we mean the movement of birds south in the fall and north in the spring, or moving from lowlands to highlands, or from the interior to the seacoasts.

We can have a pretty good idea as to why it's good for the birds to migrate. For example, they go to warmer climates because some of them couldn't survive winter conditions. Those birds that feed on certain insects, or small rodents, wouldn't find any food in winter. Oddly enough, temperature alone wouldn't make most birds migrate. Did you know that your canary could probably survive outside in the winter in temperatures 50 degrees below zero, Fahrenheit, if it had enough food?

Whatever the reason for the migration (and there are many), how do birds know when it's time to take off on their long flights? Well, we know that they migrate quite punctually every year when the season is changing. And what is the surest, unmistakable clue to the fact that the season is changing? The length of the day! It is believed that birds can tell when the days get shorter (and longer in the spring), and this is the best "alarm clock" they have to tell them to get along!

Since birds breed in the summer, this is also connected with migration. Only in this case, it's migration northward. Certain glands in the bird begin to secrete chemicals that have to do with breeding. This happens in the spring. The bird feels the need to breed and heads north where it will be summer.

So the change in the length of days and the disappearance of food tell the bird to head to warmer places. And the breeding instinct in the spring tells them to head north. There are many other factors involved, of course, and many things we still don't understand, but these are certainly among the chief clues to bird migration.

---

In the late summer, many birds in various parts of the world leave their homes and fly south for the winter. Sometimes they travel to other continents, thousands of miles away. Next spring, these birds return not only to the same country, but often to the very same nest in the same building! How do they find their way?

## HOW DO MIGRATING BIRDS FIND THEIR WAY?

Various interesting experiments have been made to try to find the answer. In one of these, a group of storks was taken from their nests before the time of the autumn migration and moved to another place. From this new location, they would have to travel in a new direction to reach their winter feeding grounds. But when the time came, they took off in exactly the same direction they would have followed from their old home! It seems as if they have an inborn instinct that tells them to fly off in a certain direction when winter approaches.

The ability of birds to find their way home is equally amazing. Birds have been taken by airplane from their home to places 400 miles away. When they were set free, they flew back to their home!

To say they have an instinct to "go home" doesn't really explain the mystery. How do they find their way? We know that young birds are not taught the road by their parents, because often the parents fly off first on the annual migrations. And birds who fly home often fly by night, so they can't see landmarks to guide them. Other birds fly over water, where there are no landmarks of any kind.

One theory is that birds can sense the magnetic fields that surround the earth. Magnetic lines of force stretch from the north to the south magnetic poles. Perhaps the birds direct themselves by these lines. But this theory has never been proven.

The fact is, science just doesn't have a full explanation of how birds find their way when they migrate or fly home! An interesting bit of history is related to the migration of birds. When Columbus was approaching the American continent, he saw great flocks of birds flying to the southwest. This meant land was near, so he changed his direction to the southwest to follow the direction taken by the birds. And that's why he landed in the Bahamas, instead of on the Florida coast!

---

## HOW FAR DO BIRDS MIGRATE?

Everybody knows that birds migrate. In fact, people use the disappearance and then the re-appearance of certain birds as a sort of way of telling the change of seasons. But no one fully understands why birds make such long journeys.

We cannot explain it by difference of temperature alone. The feathery coats birds have could protect them very well against the cold. Of course, as cold weather comes there is a lack of food for the birds, and this may explain their flight to places where it can be found. But then why do they migrate north again in the spring? Some experts think there is a connection between the change in the climate and the breeding instinct.

For whatever reason they migrate, birds certainly are the champions of all migrating animals. And the champions among the birds are the arctic terns. These amazing birds will travel in the course of a year, going back and forth, as much as 22,000 miles!

The tern nests over a wide range, from the Arctic Circle to as far south as Massachusetts. It takes this bird about 20 weeks to make its trip down to the antarctic region, and it averages about 1,000 miles a week.

Most land birds make rather short hops during their migrations. But one bird, the American golden plover, makes a long nonstop flight over the open ocean. It may fly from Nova Scotia directly to South America, a distance of about 2,400 miles over water without a stop!

Do birds start and end their migrations on exactly the same day each year? A great deal has been written about this and many people believe it happens. But no birds actually begin their migration the same day each year, though there are some who come pretty close to it. The famous swallows of Capistrano, California, are supposed to leave on October 23 and return on March 19. Despite all the publicity about it, their date of departure and arrival has been found to vary from year to year.

---

No bird has been written about so much by poets as the nightingale. Its song is supposed to be the most beautiful of all and nobody has been quite able to describe it. As a matter of fact, this attempt at

## DOES THE NIGHTINGALE SING ONLY AT NIGHT?

describing it goes back to Aristophanes, the ancient Greek writer!

According to the poets, the nightingale sings only at night and at almost any season of the year. But this isn't true. The nightingale is a migratory bird and in England, for example, can only be heard between the middle of April and the middle of June. The nightingale does not visit Ireland, Wales, or Scotland. On the continent of Europe it is quite abundant in the south, and even goes as far as Iran, Arabia, Abyssinia, Algeria, and the Gold Coast of Africa.

Only the male nightingale sings. His melody is the song of courtship to his mate, which remains silent in a neighboring bush or tree. He sings during the day as well as at night, but because of other birds, his song is not noticed so much then.

The male keeps singing until the female has hatched out her brood.

Then he remains quiet so as not to attract enemies to the nest. He stays on guard, and his notes are short calls to tell his mate that all is well, or to warn her of some danger.

While the nightingale sings one of the most beautiful songs of all birds, its plumage is very inconspicuous. Male and female are very much alike—a reddish-brown above and dull grayish-white beneath.

The nest the nightingles build is somewhat unusual. It is placed on or near the ground. The outside of the nest consists mostly of dead leaves set up vertically. In the midst of this is a deep cuplike hollow, neatly lined with fibers from roots. It is very loosely constructed and a very slight touch can disturb it. There are from four to six eggs of a deep olive color.

---

For thousands of years, the owl has been a creature to which people have attached special significance. Primitive people have many superstitions about the owl, chiefly because of the peculiar cries it makes.

## HOW CAN AN OWL SEE AT NIGHT?

In many parts of Europe when an owl is heard to hoot, it is considered a sign of death. In ancient Greece, the owl was a symbol of wisdom.

Owls of one species or another are found in all parts of the world. In the frozen arctic districts, owls have snowy-white plumage which blends in with their surroundings and keeps them safe from their enemies. In parts of Texas there are owls so tiny they are no bigger than a sparrow, and they feed on grasshoppers and beetles.

The owl is a bird that really comes to life at night, and its whole body is especially suited to this kind of life. First, let's take the owl's hoot. When the owl utters this cry in the night, creatures who may be nearby are frightened by the sound. If they make any motion or sound, the owl hears them instantly with its sensitive ears.

The ears of an owl have a flap on the outside, unlike most other birds. Some owls have a kind of "trumpet" of feathers near the ears to help them hear better. Once the owl has startled its prey and heard its motion, it can see it even in the dark! There are two reasons for this remarkable ability. The eyeballs of the owl are elastic. It can focus them instantly for any distance. The owl can also open the pupil of its eye very wide. This enables it to make use of all the night light there is.

The owl's eyes are placed so that it has to turn its whole head to change the direction of its glance.

Even the owl's feathers help it to hunt its food. The feathers are so soft that the owl can fly noiselessly and thus swoop right down on the animals it hunts. Some owls are helpful to farmers because they destroy rats, insects, and other enemies of crops. But there are other owls that are fond of chickens and other domestic fowl, and these owls cost the farmer quite a bit of money!

---

One of the strangest-looking of all birds is the toucan. In fact, it's a kind of freak among birds.

To begin with, the toucan has an enormous bill, actually larger

## WHAT IS A TOUCAN?

than its head! In some toucans, the bill is a third of the length of the entire bird. This bill is shaped like a great lobster claw and is marked with bright colors.

If you were to see a toucan, you would wonder how this bird can maintain its balance with such a bill. The answer is that the bill is very light for its size. It is paper-thin on the outside, and it's reinforced on the inside with a honeycomb of bone. At its base, this bill is as large as the head of the bird. It has an irregular toothed or cutting surface along the edge.

The tongue of the toucan is also very unusual. It has side notches and is flat and featherlike. Another peculiar thing about the toucan is the way the tail is joined to the body. It seems to have a ball and socket joint. The toucan can give this tail a jerk and raise it above its back.

The toucan is a tropical American bird that has a family of its own. It is related to such birds as the jacamars, puffbirds, barbets, and distantly to the woodpeckers. There are about 37 different species of toucans, the largest of which are about 24 inches in length.

The toucan's appetite nearly equals its bill. It eats almost anything, and in captivity it has been trained to the most varied diet. At home in the forest it turns with equal greediness to fruits, or to the eggs and young of smaller birds. When feeding, it makes a chattering noise with its great bill. It also has a harsh, unmusical cry.

The toucans live together in small flocks in the depths of the Central and South American forests. Little is known of their life history, but it is believed that they make nests in the hollows of trees. Toucans are easily tamed and thrive in captivity.

---

One of the most spectacular sights presented by any bird is that of the peacock displaying his feathers. As you might imagine, such a sight has always impressed people. In fact, in ancient times, both the Greeks and

**WHY DOES THE PEACOCK RAISE HIS FEATHERS?**

the Romans considered the peacock to be a sacred bird. But this didn't prevent the Romans from serving peacocks for dinner!

The peacock is a native of Asia and the East Indies, from which it has been brought to other parts of the world. There are only two species of peacock, and they are related to the pheasant.

Because of the way the peacock displays his feathers and struts around, a common expression has arisen: "Vain as a peacock." Actually, this is quite unfair to the peacock. It is no more vain than many other birds during the mating season.

The male peacock's display of gorgeous plumage is for the sake of the hen and for her alone. Among birds, as you know, it is the male who usually has the brighter colors and more "flashy" appearance. The peacock happens to have more marvelous colors than any other birds.

His head, neck, and breast are a rich purple, splashed with tints of green and gold. His head is also set off with a crest of 24 feathers in paler hues. His back is green, with the wing feathers tipped with copper.

The most remarkable feature of the male peacock of course is the train, or extension of his tail. A peacock is about 7 or 8 feet long, of which the tail takes up between 3 or 4 feet.

The tail is a medley of blue and green and gold. Here and there in the regular pattern are "eyes" which change colors. The train is raised and held up by the stiff quills of the shorter, true tail.

The female peacock, the peahen, is slightly smaller and quieter in tone. She has no train, and only a short crest of dull color. She usually lays ten eggs, of a dirty-brown color. Peacocks are generally kept for ornament and for the sake of their plumage.

---

Many people imagine that this strange bird lives wherever it is cold, near the North Pole, South Pole, and so on. But the penguin inhabits only the Southern Hemisphere. Penguins live along the Antarctic (not

## WHERE DO PENGUINS LIVE?

Arctic!) continent and islands. They are found as far north as Peru or southern Brazil, southwest Africa, New Zealand, and southern Australia.

The penguin is famous, of course, because it is like a comic version of a human being. Penguins stand up straight and flat-footed. Often they arrange themselves in regular files, like soldiers. When they walk, their manner seems so dignified and formal that it looks funny to us. Their plumage covers their entire bodies and is made of small, scalelike feathers. It looks like a man's evening dress of black coat and white shirt front.

The penguin that existed in prehistoric times was six feet tall, and you can imagine the effect that penguin would have on us today! There are 17 species of penguins in existence today, and the largest of these, the emperor penguin, stands about 3½ feet high and weighs about 80 pounds.

Ages ago, the penguin could fly as well as any other bird. But today its wings are short flappers, of no value at all in flying. How did this happen? One of the reasons, strangely enough, is that the penguin had few, if any, enemies. It lived in such remote areas in the Antarctic regions, that there was practically no one around to attack it. So it could safely spend all its time on land or in the water.

As generations of penguins were born and died without ever using their wings, those wings in time became very small and stiff, until today they are useless for flying. But the penguins became wonderful swimmers and divers, and those wings make excellent paddles! Penguins also developed a thick coat of fat to protect them from the icy cold of the regions where they lived.

Penguins are hunted by men today for this fat, and it may be necessary to pass laws to protect them from extinction.

Even though the sea horse is a fish, there is very little about it to suggest a fish. It has a head shaped like a pony. Instead of scales, the body of a sea horse is encased in rigid plates and thorny spikes. And its tail is like a snake's!

## WHAT IS A SEA HORSE?

The sea horse doesn't even behave like other fish. It usually curls its tail around a bit of seaweed in the water so that it won't be swept away by the current. When it does swim, it moves about with the help of a single fin which is located on its back, and it moves upright through the water.

The mouth of a sea horse is a pipe-like tube through which it sucks in its food. Unlike other fish, it has a distinct neck and movable horse-like head, which is set at an angle to its body.

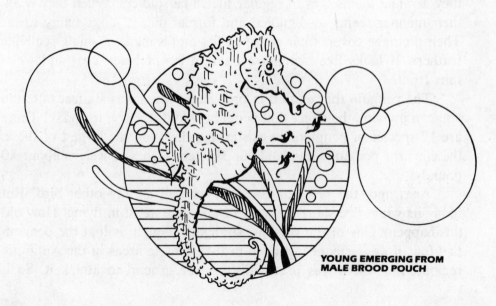

YOUNG EMERGING FROM
MALE BROOD POUCH

Perhaps the most peculiar thing about sea horses is the way they care for their young. The female fish, when she lays her eggs, puts them into the broad pouch beneath the tail of the male. So the father, instead of the mother, carries the eggs about until they hatch. Even after the young hatch out, they remain in the father's pouch for a time until they are able to take care of themselves.

Sea horses can be found in nearly all the warm and temperate seas. They belong to the pipefish family, and their food consists of small sea creatures and the eggs of other fishes. A sea horse never eats a dead thing.

There are about 50 different kinds or species of sea horses. Their size may range from 2 to 12 inches. The sea horse found along the Atlantic Coast of North America is usually about 6 inches long.

Sea horses are seen only in the summer and they are known as summer fishes. Nobody knows what happens to them in the winter!

Even though the sea horse hasn't many ways of defending itself against its enemies, it is quite safe from attack. It seems that other fishes in the sea just don't like to eat or attack sea horses!

---

The starfish is one of the most curious of sea creatures. Among its queer relatives are the prickly sea-urchins, the sea cucumbers, and the sand dollars. There are more than 6,000 of these relatives and they are called

## DOES A STARFISH HAVE EYES?

"echinoderms," which means spiny-skinned.

The starfish and its relatives all have well-developed nervous and digestive systems. This system follows the same five-armed arrangement which occurs in all echinoderms. The starfish are sometimes divided into three groups. There are the brittle stars, which break off their long snaky rays if they are caught. Their arms may extend 8 to 10 inches. There are the feather stars, whose waving rays resemble little plumes. And there are the ordinary sea stars which usually measure about 5 inches.

The tough, leathery skin of a starfish is covered with very short spines. In the center of their bodies, on both the upper and undersides, are button-shaped disks. Through these disks they draw in or expel sea water. The disks on the under sides act as mouths. The eyes are at the tips of their arms and are protected by a circle of spines.

Along the underside of their arms are grooves, and along these grooves are arranged little tubelike sucker feet. These are used both for moving about and as organs of smell. Sea stars cannot travel very fast with their little tube feet, but they can do something more remarkable. They can open an oyster! They attach the sucking disks of their feet to either half of the oyster shell and pull at it until the oyster finally opens. Then the starfish turns its stomach inside out, brings it through its mouth, and wraps it about the oyster.

Starfish can also eat by taking food into their mouths in the ordinary way. They can also replace broken arms. They may even grow a whole new body from one arm!

If you have ever been near the sea and walked along the shore where there are piers, rocks, and breakwater walls, then you've almost certainly seen barnacles. In fact, the "crust" you saw that was formed on the piers

## WHAT ARE BARNACLES?

and rocks was made up of millions and millions of barnacles!

A barnacle is simply a small shellfish. When barnacles are hatched, they swim about freely. But when they reach adult state, they no longer move about. They attach themselves to any convenient surface and actually lose their power of locomotion.

This habit of attaching to a surface, since it is done by millions of barnacles at a time, is quite a nuisance to man. For example, when barnacles form a crust on the hull of a ship, they can cut down its speed by 50 per cent! In the days of smaller ships, barnacles were a real danger because they made steering very difficult and could delay a ship from reaching its port for quite a while.

The pirates who sailed the Caribbean Sea had to tip over their ships on beaches and scrape off the barnacles. Many an old-time whaler could hardly get home after a two-year cruise because of the masses of barnacles clinging to its hull. Even today, with our modern, powerful ships, barnacles cost the world's shipping industry about a hundred million dollars a year because of the loss of time and wear and tear on machinery.

There are many different varieties of barnacles, among them the rock barnacles, which prefer to live on rocks rather than on wood or iron. As we said, when first hatched they resemble tiny crabs or lobsters and can move around. But once a barnacle attaches itself to a surface, it's for life!

An attached barnacle begins to grow a shell which encloses its body completely. The only thing that moves from then on is tentacles or antennae of the barnacle. There are six pairs of these feathery tentacles and they are able to move about to reach and draw in smaller water creatures for food.

---

The ancestor of the goldfish is the carp. In the lakes and rivers of China and Japan, the greenish-gray carp is found in great quantities, and this is where the goldfish was first developed.

## WHAT IS THE ORIGIN OF THE GOLDFISH?

The Chinese have been breeding goldfish for centuries, and the Japanese have raised goldfish for more than 400 years! Goldfish weren't known to Europe until a few were brought over about 200 years ago. These were given to Madame Pompadour of the court of King Louis XV of France. Because she was the leader of fashion, other people began importing them.

Goldfish vary in size from 1½ inches to about 12 inches. The common goldfish, the fantail, the comet, and the nymph, are the breeds best known to the Western world. The common goldfish has a slender body and rather short, tough fins.

The fantail has a shorter, fatter body with double tail and fins. The American-bred comet is slender, with a long, single, deeply forked and free-flowing tail. The nymph is like the comet but has a short, round body.

All these breeds may be kept in an aquarium, and millions of people have them in their homes. If you would like to keep goldfish, there are certain things you should know about them and their care.

The lowering of the back fin of a fish is a sure sign that it is not in good condition. A fungus disease, caused by plant parasites, is also common. In this, a white scum develops on the fins of the fish and extends over the body. If this scum reaches the gills, it keeps the fish from breathing and kills it.

This disease can be cured by giving the fish a salt-water bath, which will also correct the lowered-fin condition. One tablespoon of salt to a gallon of water the same temperature as that in the aquarium may be used for a daily 30-minute bath. The fish should be placed in a shallow basin containing this solution and set in a dim light.

Then the aquarium and plants should be soaked for four hours in a very weak solution of potassium permanganate, washed, and filled with a fresh supply of clean water. In two, or three days, the fish may be put back into it.

---

Did you ever eat a dish of fried scallops? As you looked at the little squares of food on your plate, did you wonder why you had never seen them in the water? What kind of creature was this that existed in square chunks of meat?

## WHAT IS A SCALLOP?

Actually, what are sold as "scallops" and what you eat as "scallops" are only the large muscles of certain mollusks. These muscles are used to open and close the shells, and they are the only part we eat.

The scallop itself is a curious creature. As you probably know, most bivalves (mollusks with two shells) find a place to live and stay there. They may fasten themselves to rocks or to timbers, or form a bed on the bottom of the ocean as the oysters do. But the scallop is quite different.

The scallop likes to wander about. He is constantly moving from place to place. The way he moves is by sucking water into his shell and then squirting it out suddenly. This gives him enough force to push himself forward in zigzag fashion.

Did you know that the scallop became a symbol for travelers because it is always moving? In the Middle Ages, pilgrims wore a scallop shell in their hats to indicate that they had made a long trip by sea.

Scallops belong to the great group of mollusks which includes snails, clams, and oysters. There are more than two hundred different species of scallops. The kind that are caught in New England waters and which we enjoy eating are chiefly the common scallop and the giant scallop. The common scallop lives in bays close to shore, and measures up to 3 inches across. The giant scallop is a sea scallop. It is found offshore in deeper waters and measures about 6 inches across.

The octopus belongs to a group of animals called "cephalopods." The name means "head-footed" because the foot is divided into long armlike tentacles that grow out around the head. The octopus has eight such tentacles.

## HOW DOES AN OCTOPUS MOVE?

Even though the octopus belongs to that part of the animal kingdom known as mollusks, it is quite different from clams and oysters, which are mollusks, too. It is more closely related to the squids.

None of these has shells. They have only a soft mantle to enclose the body. The tentacles are long and flexible with rows of suckers on the underside. These enable the octopus to grab and hold very tightly to anything it catches.

In the back part of the body of the octopus is a funnel-siphon. Water comes into this siphon and the octopus extracts oxygen from it the way a fish does. The siphon is also the way it manages to move swiftly. The octopus can shoot a stream of water from this siphon with such force that it propels itself backward very rapidly. That is the way it can get away from an enemy that comes too quickly to allow it the chance to crawl over the rocks or into crevices by means of its eight tentacles.

When an octopus lies quietly, the tentacles rest spread out over the floor of the shallow pool. Should an enemy approach, it will either escape or grab the enemy tightly. If things grow too serious, it can throw up a "smoke screen" and escape. From a sac in the lower back

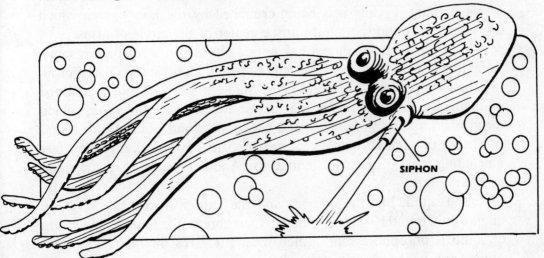

SIPHON

part of its body it can throw out a black inky fluid that clouds the surrounding water.

Also, an octopus can change color to match its surroundings. It can go from red to gray, yellow, brown, or blue-green.

---

In the days when Columbus sailed the seas there were stories told of long-armed monsters that reached out of the water to scuttle ships and pull the sailors down to the depths of the ocean. Such stories were exaggerations. There never were such monsters, and what the sailors probably saw were giant octopuses or giant squid.

## WHAT IS A SQUID?

Both of these creatures are mollusks, or shellfish. They belong to the class called "Cephalopoda." This name means "head-footed," because the foot is divided into long armlike tentacles that grow out around the head.

A typical squid has a long, slender body edged by triangular fins, a short square head with well-developed eyes, and ten arms. On the undersurface of the arms or tentacles, are arranged rows of suckers which are strengthened with tough horny rings. Two of these tentacles are longer and more flexible than the others. The suckers are concentrated at the extremity of the tentacles as a sort of "hand."

The two long tentacles are used by the squid to capture its prey. The other eight are used to transfer the food to the mouth of the squid. or for holding it while it is being crunched by the horny jaws, which are situated around the mouth in the center of the circle of arms.

Deep under the mantle, or skin, lies a horny growth which is something like a shell. This has replaced the true shell which the squid probably had at one time. There are many different kinds of squids, and one of them, the giant squid, is the largest invertebrate on earth, which means the largest animal without a backbone. Some giant squids found in the North Atlantic have been measured to have a length of 52 feet (including the outstretched tentacles). Another group of giant squid measure 7 feet.

The squid, like the octopus and the cuttlefish, can discharge an inklike fluid into the water to hide its whereabouts. One interesting group of squid is phosphorescent, which means it gives off light. The light organs are on the mantle, arms, inside the mantle cavity, and around the eyes. When seen at night, they appear quite beautiful. Other squid, called "flying squid," are able to leap across the surface of the water.

A catfish might say to you: "why do you call them 'whiskers?' They're not whiskers at all!" And, of course, it's only because those things on the fish's mouth resemble a cat's whiskers that we call them that. Actu-

## WHY DO CATFISH HAVE WHISKERS?

ally they are barbels, or feelers, and help the catfish know what's going on all about him.

There's another way a catfish is supposed to resemble a cat: it makes a buzzing or croaking sound when caught that suggests a cat's purring. It's for these two reasons that this kind of fish got its name, "catfish."

Young boys are especially well acquainted with the catfish because it's one of the easiest fish to catch. It will bite at almost any bait, from a piece of red string to a worm. And because the catfish does such a good job of caring for its young and protecting its nest, there always seems to be a lot of catfish around.

Actually, the catfish family has about 2,000 different species. The European catfish is known to grow to a length of 10 feet and a weight of 400 pounds! Some specimens of the great Mississippi catfish and the Great Lakes catfish have been found to weigh 150 pounds.

The catfishes known as the mud cat, the yellow cat, and the

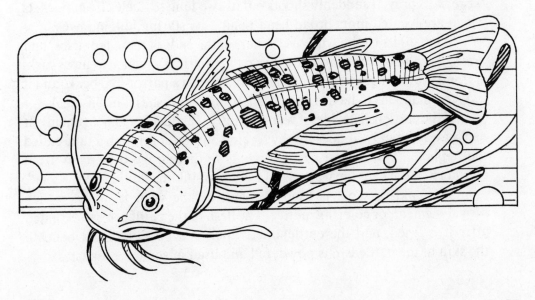

bashaw catfish are found in all large rivers of the West and South. Many catfish are good eating, especially the white cat, found in the waters of the Chesapeake Bay and the Potomac River; the blue cat, found in Southern streams; and the bullheads, bull pouts, or horned pouts.

Some catfish have strange habits. One South American species is said to travel overland from pond to pond, and another builds a nest of blades of grass for its young. There is even an electric catfish in Africa which can give a painful electric shock. In the river Nile is a species which avoids the notice of its enemies by swimming with its black belly up and its white back down!

---

Anybody who owns a canary probably knows about "cuttlebone," which comes from the cuttlefish. The cuttlebone is given to canaries and other cage birds so they can sharpen their beaks on it.

## WHAT IS A CUTTLEFISH?

But, except for this, the cuttlefish is quite unknown to most of us. The cuttlefish is not a fish, but a mollusk. It belongs to the class of mollusks called "cephalopods," which means "head-footed animals." This is because of the arrangement of the arms, or feet, around the mouth. The octopus also belongs to this class of mollusk.

The cuttlefish is a rather remarkable creature. It travels smoothly and silently through the water by moving the row of fins which are fastened to its shield-shaped body. Sometimes when it moves, it erects the first pair of its tentacles, or feelers. When it comes within striking distance of its prey, it suddenly shoots out its two long tentacles from pockets which are located in its broad head behind its staring bulging eyes.

It grasps its victim with the suckers at the ends of these tentacles, and draws it within reach of four shorter pairs of arms, which also have suckers, and are arranged around its head. It also has a parrot-like beak, and if its victim happens to have a hard shell, it simply crushes it in this beak.

If the cuttlefish decides it wants to retreat suddenly from an enemy, it backs away quickly. It does this by forcing out water through a tube called the "siphon." Sometimes, when it wants to discourage the enemy from chasing it, it darkens the water with a cloud of inkline fluid called "sepia."

This inklike sepia is used by man, by the way; it makes a rich brown pigment, or coloring matter. The flesh of the cuttlefish can be eaten after it is dried, and the cuttlebone, which is a bonelike shell beneath the skin of the cuttlefish, is powdered and used in some toothpastes.

# CHAPTER 3
# THE
# HUMAN BODY

Hormones are secreted by the endocrine glands. Endocrine means "the internal secretion of a gland." Another name for them is ductless glands, because they don't send their secretions into ducts but directly into the bloodstream. Hormones are also pro-

**WHAT IS A HORMONE?**

duced by some organs such as the liver and the kidney, but most of the hormones in the body come from glands.

Each of the various hormones produces its own special effect in the body. In general, the job of the hormones is to regulate the internal activities of the body, such as growth and nutrition, the storage and use of food materials, and the reproductive processes. If the glands produce too much or not enough, a person may have an abnormal physical appearance.

Here are what some of the chief glands and hormones do in our bodies: The thyroid gland, located in the neck, produces a hormone which helps in the growth, development, and metabolic processes of the body.

The pituitary gland, located at the base of the skull, has two parts. As we know, one hormone produced by one part of this gland has the job of promoting growth.

Another part of the pituitary gland produces two hormones which help control our use of water, fat, our blood pressure, and the way we regulate the heat in our body.

There are two important glands located at the upper end of each kidney. One produces a hormone called adrenalin. This hormone is related to blood pressure and reactions to emotion and emergencies. When you become excited or frightened, you produce more of this hormone.

Other glands in the body produce hormones which have to do with making you act like a boy or a girl. So you see that hormones are responsible for a great deal about you and your health.

---

In the body of an adult human being, there are about six quarts of blood. Floating about in this liquid there are approximately 25 billion blood cells!

## HOW DOES THE BODY MAKE BLOOD CELLS?

It is almost impossible for us to imagine such a tremendous quantity, but this might give you an idea. Each blood cell is so tiny that it can only be seen under a microscope. If you could make a string of these microscopic cells, that string would go four times around the earth!

Where do these cells come from? Obviously, the "factory" that turns out such an enormous quantity of cells must have amazing productive power — especially when you consider that sooner or later every one of these cells disintegrates and is replaced by a new one!

The birthplace of the blood cells is the bone marrow. If you look at an opened bone, you can see the reddish-grey, spongy marrow in the cavity of the bone. If you look at it under a microscope, you can see a whole network of blood vessels and connective-tissue fibers. Between these and blood vessels are countless marrow cells, and the blood cells are born in these marrow cells.

When the blood cell lives in the bone marrow, it is a genuine cell with a nucleus of its own. But before it leaves the bone marrow for the blood stream, it loses the nucleus. As a result, the ripe blood cell is no longer a complete cell. It is not really a living structure any longer, but a kind of mechanical apparatus.

The blood cell is like a balloon made of protoplasm, and filled with the blood pigment hemoglobin, which makes it red. The sole function of the blood cell is to combine with oxygen in the lungs, and to exchange the oxygen for carbon dioxide in the tissues.

The number and size of the blood cells in a living creature depend on its need for oxygen. Worms have no blood cells. Cold-blooded amphibians have large and relatively few cells in their blood. Animals that are small, warm-blooded, and live in mountainous regions have the most blood cells.

The human bone marrow adapts itself to our needs for oxygen. At high altitudes, it produces more cells; at low altitudes, less. People living on a mountain top may have almost twice as many blood cells as people living along the seacoast!

---

The blood which flows through the arteries, capillaries, and veins of your body contains many different materials and cells. Each part of the blood has its own special work and importance.

## WHY IS OUR BLOOD RED?

There is, first of all, the liquid part of the blood. This is called the plasma, and makes up a little more than half the blood. It is light yellow and a little thicker than water because many substances are dissolved in it.

What are some of these substances? — Proteins, antibodies that fight disease, fibrinogen that helps the blood to clot, carbohydrates, fats, salts, and so on, in addition to the blood cells.

The red cells (also called red blood corpuscles) give the blood its color. There are so many of them in the blood that it all looks red. There are about 35 trillion of these tiny, round, flat discs moving around in your body all at once! And they stay in the blood vessels at all times.

As the young red cell grows and takes on adult form in the marrow, it loses its nucleus and builds up more and more hemoglobin. Hemoglobin is the red pigment, or color. It contains iron combined with protein.

As the blood passes through the lungs, oxygen joins the hemoglobin of the red cells. The red cells carry the oxygen through the arteries and capillaries to all cells of the body. Carbon dioxide from the body cells is returned to the lungs through the veins in the same way, combined mainly with hemoglobin.

Red cells live only about four months and then are broken up, mostly in the spleen. New red cells are always being formed to replace the cells that are worn out and destroyed.

In addition to the red blood cells, there are also several kinds of white blood cells.

You can see that blood, so necessary for life, is not a simple thing. Many different substances have their special work and importance.

Although the red cells are by far more numerous in the blood and give blood its color, the white blood cells have a critical role, too. The white blood cells are called leucocytes.

## WHAT DO WHITE BLOOD CELLS DO?

The most common leucocytes are granular cells. These cells pass in and out of the blood to the spot where germs or injured tissue have collected. Some of these cells, called neutrophiles, take bacteria into themselves and destroy them. They also give off substances which digest and soften dead tissue and form pus.

Other white cells in the blood are called lymphocytes. The lymphocytes often increase in numbers in a part of the body where infection has continued for more than a short time. This is a part of the body's process for fighting infections, so you can see their job is quite important.

Still other white blood cells are the monocytes. These cells, together with other cells in the tissues, have the ability to take up pieces of dead material. They can also surround material such as dirt, and keep it from coming in contact with healthy tissue cells.

By the way, even though white blood cells are so necessary to the body, too many of them are not good either. When too many white blood cells are formed, and they do not grow into the healthy, active cells that are needed, the condition is called leukemia, or cancer of the blood.

So the blood is like a chemical formula in which there has to be just the right amount of each substance — red cells, white cells, proteins, salts, carbohydrates, fats, and so on.

---

There is no transportation system in any city that can compare in efficiency with the circulatory system of the body.

If you will imagine two systems of pipes, one large and one small, both meeting at a central pumping station, you'll have an idea of the circulatory system. The smaller system of pipes goes from the heart to the lungs and back. The larger one goes from the heart to the various other parts of the body.

## HOW DO ARTERIES DIFFER FROM VEINS?

These pipes are called arteries, veins, and capillaries. Arteries are

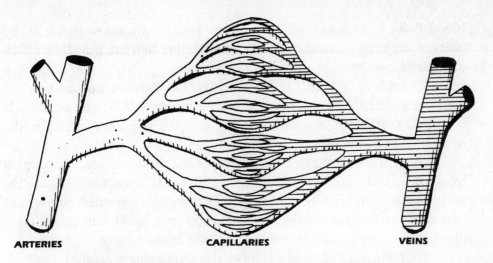

ARTERIES                    CAPILLARIES                 VEINS

blood vessels in which blood is going away from the heart. In veins, the blood is coming back to the heart. In general, arteries are carrying pure blood to various parts of the body; and the veins are bringing back blood loaded with waste products. The capillaries are tiny vessels for conducting blood from arteries to veins. The pumping station is the heart.

Arteries lie deep in the tissues, except at the wrist, over the instep, at the temple, and along the sides of the neck. At any of these places, the pulse can be felt, and a doctor can get an idea of the condition of the arteries.

The largest arteries have valves where they leave the heart. These vessels are made of many elastic muscles which can expand and contract. Arterial blood is bright red in color and moves through the arteries in spurts.

Veins lie closer to the surface of the skin; the blood in them is darker and flows more evenly; and they have valves at intervals all along their course.

---

There are all kinds of big roads and highways connecting big cities so that food and other necessary materials can reach them. But what about the small towns and little villages? They need food and supplies, too.

## WHAT ARE CAPILLARIES?

The little roads and byways that reach the small towns and villages are like the capillaries in the human body. As we know, blood is pumped out of the heart to all parts of the body and the big vessels through which this blood flows are known as the arteries. But far from the heart, in all parts of the body, these big vessels become tiny hairlike branches called capillaries.

A capillary is 50 times thinner than the thinnest human hair! In fact, the average diameter of a capillary is about 1/3,000 of an inch. It is so thin that blood corpuscles pass through a capillary in single file, which means blood passes through the capillaries very slowly.

About 700 capillaries could be packed into the space occupied by a pin. Each capillary is about 1/50 of an inch long. Since the purpose of capillaries is to bring and take away needed substances to and from every part of the body, you can imagine how many millions upon millions of capillaries there are in the human body.

What happens when blood flows through a single capillary (which takes about a second)? The blood does not leave the capillary. But the wall of the capillary is very thin; it consists of only a single layer of cells. Through this wall, the blood gives up its oxygen to the surrounding tissues. In return, it receives the carbon dioxide which the tissues around the capillary have given up.

At the same time, other substances which supply nourishment to the tissues pass from the blood, and waste products enter the capillary. Eventually, the blood and the materials it has picked up are returned to the heart by way of the veins.

---

The heart, as we have learned, is a pump that sends the blood circulating through our body. The pumping action takes place when the left ventricle of the heart contracts. This forces the blood out into the arteries,

## WHAT IS BLOOD PRESSURE?

which expand to receive the oncoming blood.

But the arteries have a muscular lining which resists this pressure, and thus the blood is squeezed out of them into the smaller vessels of the body. Blood pressure is the amount of pressure on the blood as a result of the heart's pumping and the resistance of the arterial walls.

There are two kinds of pressure: maximum and minimum. The maximum pressure occurs when the left ventricle contracts; it is called the systolic pressure. The minimum pressure occurs just before the heartbeat which follows; it is called the diastolic pressure.

When your doctor measures your blood pressure, he uses an instrument which measures it in terms of a column of mercury, which rises and falls under the pressure. He reads it in millimeters rather than in inches. The average systolic pressure in a young man is about 120 millimeters (about 5 inches) of mercury. The diastolic pressure is about 80 millimeters of mercury. These figures are usually stated as 120/80, or 120 over 80.

When the blood pressure is in this range, it provides the body with a circulating supply of blood without unduly straining the walls of the blood vessels. But there are many variations from this range which may be quite normal.

With age, the blood pressure gradually rises until, at 60 years, it is about 140/87. There are many factors that affect the blood pressure. Overweight people often have a higher blood pressure than people of normal weight. Tension, exercise, and even posture may affect the blood pressure.

---

You may get a "shock" when you see your mark on a test, or you may say you're "shocked" if you see an accident. But medically speaking, this isn't shock. The word "shock" means a condition in which the

## WHAT IS SHOCK?

essential activities of the body are affected. Usually, they are slowed up.

A person in a state of shock may have a sudden or gradual feeling of weakness or faintness. He may become very pale, and the skin may feel cold and clammy. Perspiration is increased, and the pupils of the eyes become enlarged.

Shock is also accompanied by changes in the mental state. It can begin with a feeling of restlessness, and it may develop to a state of unconsciousness.

All of these are symptoms of shock. They are produced because the volume of blood in effective circulation is lowered, along with the blood pressure. As in fainting, blood going to the brain may eventually lead to unconsciousness. This lack of blood in the capillaries also explains why the skin may feel cold.

Of course, if a person has been injured so that he is losing a great deal of blood, this in itself will produce a state of shock. But shock may also be caused by undergoing great stress, by strong emotion, by pain or sudden illness, or by some accident. The important thing is that for one reason or another, the blood doesn't circulate as it should, and as a result, the essential activities of the body are affected.

The best thing to do when a person is in a state of shock is to get a doctor. Do not move the patient, have him sit up, or use a pillow under his head. Lay the person on his back if he is unconscious, and keep him warm until help comes.

---

There are many things that people sometimes claim they "see" that really aren't there. They may have visions of "ghosts" or strange creatures. Sometimes little children claim they "saw" things that no one else did. Sometimes these are fantasies or daydreams; sometimes they are illusions.

## WHAT ARE HALLUCINATIONS?

There is a difference between an illusion and an hallucination. When a person has an illusion, there is something present that stimulates the eyes or senses. It can be verified, because other people see it, too. A mirage, for example, is a kind of illusion. But the main point is that something is there that causes the person to think he saw what he saw.

When a person has a hallucination, however, nothing is there! There is no outside stimulation to the eyes or the senses. The only stimulation comes from the person himself, from his own fantasy.

Hallucinations can be of various types, relating to the various senses. The most common have to do with hearing. A person imagines he hears voices, mutterings, laughter, cries, bells ringing, music playing or even shots ringing out! The second most common type of hallucination has to do with seeing. People imagine they see certain persons who aren't there, or they may see animals, objects, or whole scenes before them. Sometimes they "see" strange, horrible, and unearthly things that terrify them. And sometimes people even have hallucinations about tastes and smells, or things they feel on their skin!

There are many reasons why people have hallucinations. One of the most common is that a person is very troubled and disturbed by something. If someone has been aroused emotionally to a high pitch, perhaps very angry or frightened, he may have hallucinations.

In other words, persons who are hallucinating are usually in a state of great excitement, fear, ecstasy, or anticipation of something. Certain drugs also cause hallucinations. Cocaine, for example, gives the hallucination of insects crawling on the skin!

Every now and then, you read in the papers about a person who has "forgotten" who he is. He remembers nobody and nothing from his past, not even his name. We say this person is suffering from amnesia.

## WHAT IS AMNESIA?

We all get emotionally upset from time to time. We feel hurt, angry, disappointed or frightened for one reason or another. When we feel such emotional pain, we want to do something about it. For example, a simple way of dealing with it is to cry, or blush, or break out in a cold sweat. In fact, these reactions happen without our control. They are considered normal reactions, since practically everyone has them.

But a person may react to emotional stress and pain in another way. Instead of facing the problems that caused him to be upset, he tries to act in such a way that he won't feel the anxiety. He "runs away" from it. He "protects" himself in this way from emotional pain.

One form of this reaction is amnesia. A person simply acts as if all those things which bothered and upset him so much didn't really happen to him but to someone else! He "forgets" his anxiety.

In forgetting this, he also forgets a great many other things that were linked to his anxiety — including who he was! He just can't remember anything about the past. But he may act quite normally about the present. He lives and works as another person, and may not attract any special attention.

Sometimes a person recovers from amnesia suddenly, of his own accord. In many cases, however, a person can be helped to recover by a psychiatrist. A curious thing is that people who recover from amnesia don't remember events which took place while they were suffering from amnesia.

Here's a sure way to win a bet! Challenge anybody you know to walk blindfolded straight down the sidewalk without going off the edge. He is sure to lose because he'll soon start walking in a circle!

## WHY DO WE WALK IN CIRCLES WHEN WE ARE LOST?

People who have been lost in a fog or in a snowstorm, have often walked for hours imagining they were heading in a straight direction. After a while, they arrived right back where they started from.

Here's the reason why we can't walk in a straight line without our eyes to guide us. Our body is asymmetrical. This means there is not a perfect balance between our right side and our left side. The heart for instance is on the left side, the liver on the right. The skeleton of our body is asymmetrical too. The spine is not perfectly straight. Our thighs and our feet are different on each side of our body. All of this means that the structure of the muscles in our body is asymmetrical, or not perfectly balanced.

Since our muscles differ from right side to left side, this affects the way we walk, our gait. When we close our eyes, the control of our gait depends on the muscles and structure of our body, and one side forces us to turn in a certain direction. We end up walking in a circle.

By the way, this is true not only of the muscles in our legs, but in our arms, too. Tests were made in which blindfolded people tried to drive a car in a straight line. In about 20 seconds, every person in the test began to drive off the road! It's a good reason for keeping your eyes wide open whether you're walking or driving!

---

In ancient times, people didn't understand diseases and what caused them. So they often behaved very cruelly to victims of certain diseases. People who had epilepsy in the Middle Ages were thought of as lunatics,

## WHAT IS EPILEPSY?

or bewitched! Yet did you know that many great people and many geniuses were epileptic? Among them were the Duke of Wellington, Richard Wagner, Vincent van Gogh, and Louis Hector Berlioz.

Epilepsy is a disease of the nervous system. People with epilepsy have sudden spells during which they have spasms called convulsions, after which they may become unconscious or fall into a coma.

Doctors cannot yet explain exactly what happens and what causes the convulsions. It seems that the normal patterns of activity of the brain become disrupted for a short time. The brain tissue in these people is sensitive to chemical changes, and when some sort of change takes place, the brain responds by sending out discharges that cause the convulsions.

A person has to be predisposed to epilepsy to have such reactions, because other people may undergo the same chemical changes and not have convulsions. There is a possibility that it is hereditary.

An epileptic attack may be caused by a head injury, a high fever, tumors, or scars in the brain substance, disturbances in the blood supply, and so on. Injury to the brain may result in epilepsy.

Epilepsy, however, has nothing to do with mental development. A person who has epilepsy should be considered a normal individual, not an invalid or some sort of outcast. Epileptics can lead normal lives — go to school, work, marry, and raise families.

Medical science has developed drugs to prevent attacks, and to control them when they do occur. These medicines are usually given to people over a period of many years, or even for a lifetime, so that they lead normal, happy lives.

---

Of all the things that distinguish man from the rest of the animal kingdom, the most important is his brain. Many of the lower animals have no brain at all, or a tiny one, or one that is poorly developed. For

## WHAT IS THE BRAIN?

instance, an earthworm has a brain about the size of a pinhead, a rabbit has a thimble-sized brain. The brain of a man weighs, on the average, about 3 pounds.

By the way, the size of the brain is not the most important thing about it. An elephant has a bigger brain than man, but it is not as well developed.

The brain has three main divisions: the cerebrum, the cerebellum, and the medulla oblongata. The cerebrum is considered the most important part. It is from here that all our voluntary actions are controlled.

The cerebrum is also the biggest part of man's brain, filling most of the space in the upper and back part of the skull. The cerebrum is divided into two equal parts or hemispheres, and its surface is covered with wrinkles and folds. This surface is composed of gray matter, made up of cells. The higher the type of animal, the more numerous and deeper are the folds. Under this surface, called the cortex, there is white matter which is made up of nerve fibers. Through this part pass the messages to and from the cortex.

Certain sections of the cortex control certain body functions, so every part of the cortex is different. Science can point to certain parts as the controls over sight, or feeling, or hearing, or movement of certain muscles. That's why an injury to just one part of the brain (for instance, by a blood clot) can impair one's capacity to perform a certain function, such as speech.

The cerebellum is in the back of the skull, beneath the cerebrum. It controls the power of balancing and the co-ordination of the muscles. If it is injured, a man may not be able to walk in a straight line or stand erect.

The medulla oblongata is about the size of the end of the thumb and is found at the end of the spinal cord. It controls breathing, the beating of the heart, digestion, and many other activities that seem to go on by themselves. This is where the nerve fibers that go from the brain to the spinal cord cross. One side of the brain controls the other side of the body. The right half of the cerebrum, for example, controls the left leg, and so on.

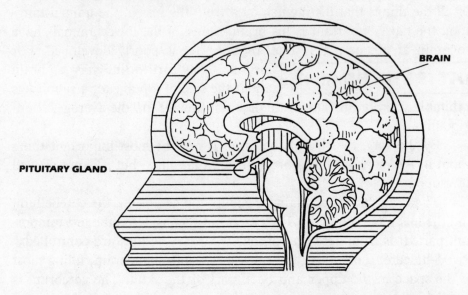

BRAIN

PITUITARY GLAND

Can you recite the alphabet easily and quickly? Can you write your name easily? Can you play the scale on a musical instrument?

You would probably say that you memorized all this. But what

## WHAT IS MEMORY?

you actually did was to learn them. And the way you learned them was by forming a habit! In other words, what was once quite difficult for you, such as reciting the alphabet or playing the scale, became easy and almost automatic when you formed a habit of doing it. So memory can be described as learning by means of forming habits.

A human being has a tremendous number of such habits that enable him to do most of the ordinary things in life, such as fastening a button or washing the hands. But suppose you read a book and someone asked you what the book was about, or to describe the plot. Surely, this cannot be called a habit.

But if you examine the situation carefully, you will see that something very much like habit does play a part. For example, in ordinary habits, you learn how to put certain elements together in the proper order. Now, when you give the plot of a book, or tell what it's about, you are doing the same kind of thing. In fact, some psychologists say that all learning (and this also means memory) is made up of a vast combination of simple habits.

But this doesn't mean that in learning and remembering you simply form habits by mechanically going through the motions of practice, or repeating them. There are several other things that enter into the situation and make it possible for you to learn and remember better.

One of these is the will to learn, or the motive or incentive. Another important thing is understanding what one is learning. For example, you will learn (or memorize) a poem more quickly when you understand it. And you will remember it longer, too.

Still another important help in learning and remembering is the association of new ideas with ideas you have already stored away in your memory.

---

Most of us think that every action we take is voluntary — that we sit down and stand up because we want to, or shake hands because we want to, and so on.

## WHAT IS INSTINCT?

But the actions of people and all living things are really not so easily explained. For example, as you ride a bicycle, you may make dozens of motions without even thinking about them as you do them. These actions are the result of learning and experience.

Now, suppose you touch something hot and instantly draw your finger away. You didn't even think of taking your finger away — you just did it. This action is a reflex action.

Now we come to a third kind of action that takes place without thinking on your part. You are hungry. You don't always tell yourself, "I am hungry, I will look for food." You just go about getting food. This kind of action might be described as an instinct.

Whether or not human beings really have instincts (such as seeking food, caring for one's young, etc.) is something psychologists are still not agreed upon. But we know that other animals act by instinct. An instinct is an action that accomplishes a certain objective without thinking on the part of the doer.

For example, a bird building a nest gathers sticks, grass, fibers, or down. It then arranges them upon a branch or ledge in such a way that the nest has a certain height and stability, and is like the nest of other birds of the same species. The only thing that can explain such behavior is instinct.

An instinctive action is always carried on because there is some natural stimulation inside the creature (such as hunger, fear, the desire to mate). In fact, it is quite probable that the secretions of certain glands in the body cause the bird or animal to perform what we call an instinctive act. Seeking food, mating, maternal care, migration, and hibernation are all related to the actions of the glands in a bird.

Almost all living animals have some instinctive behavior to satisfy some vital need of the body.

---

When you go to the doctor, does he ask you to cross your legs and then hit your knee with a small rubber hammer?

What the doctor is testing is the reflex action. In this case, it is a

## WHAT CAUSES A REFLEX?

special reflex called the patellar reflex, because the hammer struck a ligament called the patellar ligament.

What actually happens when the hammer strikes the ligament? A stimulus passes from a sensory cell in the ligament to the spinal cord. There it is transferred to a motor cell, and this sends an action current to the muscles of the leg. The leg twitches, just as if it were about to kick an enemy in self-defense.

This action is a reflex action. In other words, it is automatic. We have no control over it because it is not an action that is started in the brain. For instance, when you go to bed and close your eyes, you are performing a voluntary act. But if a speck of dust flies into your eye, you close it immediately whether you want to or not. This automatic movement is a reflex.

So we can define a reflex as an automatic response by the body to an external stimulus, without the influence of the will.

How does this happen?—The spinal cord is the transfer point for our reflexes. When sensory cells bring in the stimulus from the skin, they go to the spinal cord and are transferred there to motor cells. These motor cells send out currents to certain muscles and make them act. The nerve impulses do not pass through the brain.

More than 90 per cent of all the actions performed by man's nervous system are reflex actions!

---

# HOW DO OUR MUSCLES WORK?

In our bodies there are certain cells which make up connective tissue—tissue that joins the various parts of the body together. All the cells in connective tissue can contract, or tighten up. In some parts of the body, these cells can contract to a special degree, so they transform themselves into muscle cells.

At those points in the body where muscle cells are used frequently, they multiply and join together to form a single smooth muscle composed of many fibers. Smooth muscles are found in many parts of the body and help many organs to function. For instance, smooth muscles contract and dilate our eyes, regulate our breathing, make our intestines function.

The fiber of smooth muscles is strong, but it is slow. So whenever rapid motion is necessary, the body has developed the smooth muscles a step further. The fibers of the smooth muscles have developed into a higher form called striated muscle. All the muscles which make our limbs move are striated.

There are 639 muscles in the human body. The muscles are really the flesh of the body, just as the red meat bought at the butcher shop is really muscle. Muscles are all sizes and have many shapes. A medium-sized muscle contains about ten million muscle cells, and the whole body contains about six billion muscle cells!

Each of these six billion muscle cells is like a motor containing ten cylinders arranged in a row. The cylinders are tiny boxes that contain fluid. A muscle contracts when the brain sends a message to these tiny boxes. For a fraction of a second, the fluid in the tiny box congeals; then it becomes a fluid again. It is this action that causes the muscle to move.

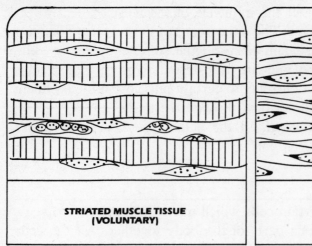

**STRIATED MUSCLE TISSUE (VOLUNTARY)**

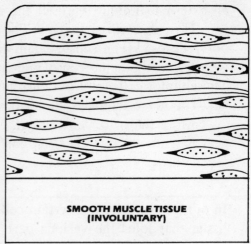

**SMOOTH MUSCLE TISSUE (INVOLUNTARY)**

The only muscles in our bodies that we can move are the striated muscles. The smooth muscles (for instance, those that control digestion) act independently of our will. When a muscle is stimulated into action, it reacts quickly. It may contract in less than one tenth of a second. But before it has time to relax, another message comes along. It contracts again and again. All these contractions take place so quickly that they become fused into one action with the result that the muscle performs a smooth, continuous action!

---

The strength of normal, healthy human bones is amazing. The saying that our bones are "twice as strong as oak" is not far from wrong.

Bone needs to be strong because it forms the framework, or skeleton, that supports the whole body. Bones vary in shape and size according to the type of animal to which they belong. Fish and small

## WHAT ARE OUR BONES MADE OF?

birds have tiny bones. Elephants have bones that weigh several hundred pounds!

All bones have similar composition. Bone is a hard, grayish-white substance, of which about two thirds are inorganic, or mineral matter, especially phosphate of lime. This gives the bone hardness, but at the same time, it makes the bone more brittle.

The remaining third of the bone is organic, or animal matter. This gives the bones the toughness which helps them resist breakage. In certain types of bones, there is a fatty substance called marrow, which is organic matter with a very high food value.

There is also a small amount of water in bone, which seems to dry out as the body grows older. As this drying takes place and as the mineral matter in the bone increases, the bones become more breakable and slower to knit and heal.

When you break a bone in your arm, for example, it must be set. This means it must be fastened firmly in its natural place so that the ends cannot move. The bone must knit before you can use your arm again.

The knitting is done by tiny cells known as osteoblasts. They secrete a limey substance that makes the bones hard and firm again. These cells also help in the natural growth of bones. Other cells called osteoclasts tear down old tissue so that growth is possible. This double process of building up and tearing down is going on in the bones all the time.

---

The average body of a human being contains about three pounds of calcium. Most of this is found in the bones. Calcium is an essential part of the structure of the bone.

## WHAT IS CALCIUM?

We might, in fact, compare the structure of a bone to reinforced concrete. The bone has certain fibers called collagen fibers which are like the flexible iron wires often embedded in concrete. Calcium forms the bed in which these bone fibers are fixed.

The calcium content of our bones changes as we grow older. During the first year, a child's bones have little calcium and great flexibility. A child can perform all kinds of contortions without breaking any bones. By the time a man is eighty, his bones may be 80 per cent calcium and break easily.

One of the reasons young children are urged to drink a great deal of milk is that milk is the ideal calcium containing food, and, of course, young bodies need plenty of calcium for their bones. One quart of cow's milk contains almost two grams of calcium. Cheese, buttermilk, and yogurt also supply great quantities of calcium.

In those parts of the country where calcium is hard to obtain, people have trouble with their teeth and often suffer from bone fractures. A frequent cause of calcium deficiency is the practice of making hard water soft by removing the calcium from it.

Hard water interferes with the lathering of soap. The calcium in hard water combines with acids and salts in the soap and produces compounds which don't dissolve.

The practice of removing calcium from hard water also has a bad effect on the foods cooked in the water. If the water has a low calcium content, foods cooked in it actually lose part of their own calcium to the water. But foods will gain in calcium content when cooked in hard water with a high calcium content.

---

Do you brush your teeth at least twice a day? If you do, and you brush hard, have you ever wondered why you don't wear your teeth down? The fact is that our teeth are pretty tough — about as hard as rocks.

## WHAT ARE OUR TEETH MADE OF?

Every tooth is made up of the same two parts: a root, or roots, to anchor it in the jaw-bone, and a crown, the part that can be seen in the mouth.

Teeth are composed mostly of mineral salts, of which calcium and phosphorus are the most prominent. The enamel is hard and shiny, and covers the crown. The cementum is a bonelike material that covers the root. The dentine is an ivorylike material that forms the bulk or body of the tooth. And the dental pulp is in a hollow space called the pulp chamber inside the tooth. The dental pulp is made up of tissue that contains nerves, arteries, and veins. These enter the tooth through an opening at or near the root end.

As you've probably noticed when you look at your teeth in the mirror, they are different in size, and in shape. In a full set of teeth, there are four types, each having a special duty. The incisors, in the center of the mouth, cut or incise food. The cuspids, which tear food, are on either side of the incisors at the corners of the mouth. They have long, heavy roots and sharp, pointed crowns.

The bicuspids, just back of the cuspids, have two points, or cusps, and one or two roots. They tear and crush food. The molars, in the back of the mouth, have several cusps and two or three roots. They grind food.

When a scientist who has been digging for fossils or other remains of ancient life turns up with some teeth, he is very happy. Teeth are an important clue as to the kind of creature it was that lived there.

## ARE OUR TEETH THE SAME AS ANIMAL TEETH?

For example, beasts of prey have tearing teeth, rodents have gnawing teeth, and cattle have grinding teeth. Every animal — whether horse, cow, mouse, cat, or dog — has teeth suitable for its way of life, its food, and even its general nature.

A beaver, for example, has great cutting teeth. The canine teeth of dogs and cats are sharp and long so that it is easy for them to seize and hold their prey. Their sharp back teeth cut up and break the flesh and bones.

A squirrel has teeth that can easily gnaw through the hard shell of a nut. Even fish have teeth that help them with their food. Some sharks have cutting teeth for eating fish, while other sharks have blunt teeth for crushing shellfish. The pike has teeth that lean backward as the prey is swallowed and then straighten up again. The teeth of snakes are set inward at an angle so that their prey cannot escape.

Man has what is known as a "collective" dentition, which means that he has many different kinds of teeth, one alongside another.

According to scientists, the structure of the human teeth is evidence that the human body is adapted to a mixed plant-and-animal diet.

---

Concentrate right now and imagine that you are about to eat a lemon. Think of yourself biting into this lemon. Do you feel the saliva beginning to flow?

## WHAT IS SALIVA?

This is one of the interesting things about our salivary glands. They don't function mechanically, but are subject to the control of the brain. There are three pairs of salivary glands. One is in front of the ear, one under the tongue, and one under the lower jaw.

The salivary glands automatically adapt the amount and nature of the saliva to the immediate task. Animals that eat moist foods have little saliva. Fish have no salivary glands, but in grain-eating birds, they are very developed. When a cow receives fresh feed, its salivary glands secrete about fifty quarts. When it receives dry hay, the quantity of saliva rises to about 200 quarts. The largest human salivary gland

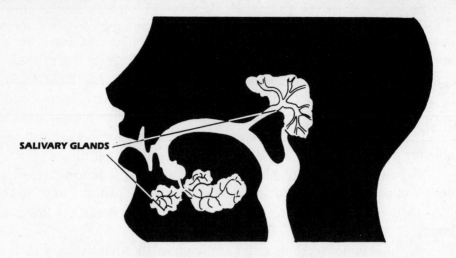

SALIVARY GLANDS

secretes about twenty-five thousand quarts of saliva in a lifetime!

Each of the salivary glands has its own special job. The largest one, the parotid gland in front of the ear, secretes large quantities of watery saliva. The chief purpose of this saliva is to dilute and to moisten the food well.

The glands near the lower jaw secrete a different kind of saliva; it makes the food "slippery."

Which of the salivary glands will produce the most saliva depends on the food we take in. If we bite into a juicy apple that doesn't have to be moistened, the lower glands will function. But if we eat a dry cracker, the parotid gland goes to work and produces large quantities of watery saliva.

Human saliva contains an enzyme known as amylase. This works on starch, splitting the molecules into dextrin and then into malt sugar.

The feeling of hunger is a message sent to your brain by your body. The message is that nutritive materials are missing from the blood. Let's see how this happens.

## WHAT MAKES US FEEL HUNGRY?

Our bodies and those of all living things must maintain a state of metabolic equilibrium. This means there has to be a certain balance and control over our intake of fuel and its use. To regulate our body weight we have thirst, hunger, and appetite.

In the brain we have a hunger center. It acts like a brake on the activities of the stomach and intestines. When the blood has sufficient nutritive materials, the hunger center stops the activities of the stomach and intestines. But when there is a lack of nutrition, the intestines and stomach become active. That's why you can hear your stomach rumbling when you're hungry.

But hunger itself has nothing to do with an empty stomach. For example, a person who is feverish may have an empty stomach but not feel hungry. His body uses up its protein supplies and feeds itself from within.

When you feel hungry, your body is crying out for fuel—any kind of fuel. A really hungry person will eat any kind of food. It is your appetite that sees to it that you choose the mixed diet that your body requires. For example, when a man sits down to dinner, one bowl of soup may be all the soup he wants. Then he goes on to meat and vegetables. When he's had enough of these, he may go on to dessert, cake, coffee. But it would be pretty hard for him to eat this same quantity of food if it all consisted of potatoes!

How long a living creature can go without food depends on its metabolism. Warm-blooded animals have a more active metabolism, and so use up their store of fuel more rapidly. The smaller and more active the animal, the more rapidly it uses up its food supplies.

---

Taste depends on the impact of the atoms given off by a substance on certain specially sensitive organs in our bodies. If the atoms of a substance can't move about freely, we can't taste it. That's why we can only taste things that are in a state of solution.

## HOW DO WE TASTE OUR FOOD?

Animals that live in water have taste buds all over their bodies. For instance, fish can taste with their tail fins! Animals that live on land have their taste buds concentrated in their mouths, and in man they exist only on the tongue.

If you examine your tongue in a mirror, you will see that it is covered with tiny, wartlike bumps, which are called papillae. The taste buds are situated in the walls of these papillae.

The number of taste buds found in animals depends on the needs of the particular species. For instance, a whale swallows whole schools of fish without chewing them; it has few taste buds, or none at all. A pig has 5,500 taste buds, a cow has 35,000, and an antelope, 50,000. Man is not by any means the most sensitive taster; he has only 3,000 taste buds!

The taste buds on the human tongue are distributed in different zones, and each zone is sensitive to a different kind of taste. The back of the tongue is more sensitive to bitter, the sides are sensitive to sour and salt, and the tip of the tongue picks up sweet tastes. In the center of the tongue, there is a zone without any taste buds, and it can taste nothing!

Smells are an important part of our tasting process. At least half of what we think of as taste is not taste at all, but really smell! This is true when we "taste" such things as coffee, tea, tobacco, wine, apples, oranges, and lemons. For instance, when we drink coffee, we first sense the warmth, then the bitterness that comes from the acid and the roasting, and then the sweetness, if it has been added. But not until the warm vapor released by the coffee hits our throat and nose and sends its messages to the brain, do we really "taste" the coffee! The proof is that if you close your nose with a clothespin, not only won't you be able to "taste" the coffee, but you'll find you can't tell the difference between two completely different things you are eating or drinking!

---

The food we take into our bodies supplies us with many important substances such as proteins, fats, carbohydrates, water, and mineral substances. But these alone are not enough. In order to maintain life

## WHY DO WE NEED VITAMIN C?

we need still other substances known as vitamins.

Vitamins are substances formed by plants or animals. They must be supplied to the body in minute quantities so that vital processes can continue undisturbed. When there is a lack of vitamins in our body, diseases will occur. For instance, lack of vitamin A affects our vision; lack of vitamin B produces a disease called beriberi, and so on.

Long before man knew about vitamins, it had been observed that when people couldn't get certain types of foods, diseases would develop. Sailors, for instance, who went on long trips and couldn't get fresh vegetables would get a disease called scurvy. In the seventeenth century British sailors were given lemons and limes to prevent this disease.

And this, by the way, is why British sailors got the nickname, "limeys!"

The vitamin that prevents scurvy is vitamin C. It is also called ascorbic acid. Some vitamins are found in the embryos of plants. For example, vitamin B, is found in the germ of the wheat. Vitamin C is found in the fresh green leaves, the roots, the stems, the buds and the pods of fully developed plants.

A curious thing about vitamin C is that almost all mammals produce their own vitamin C in the liver and so never suffer from a lack of it. But man, the apes, and guinea pigs are the only mammals which cannot produce their own vitamin C in the liver!

What happens when there is a lack of this vitamin in the body? The blood vessels become fragile and bleed easily. Black-and-blue marks appear on the skin and near the eyes. The gums bleed easily. Our hormones and enzymes don't function well, our resistance to infection by bacteria is lowered, and we may develop inflammations in the throat.

---

Wouldn't it be wonderful if people who lost an arm or a leg or even a finger in an accident could simply grow another one in its place? Human beings can't do this, but there are living creatures who can! The process by which such organisms can replace structures or organs is called regeneration.

## WHAT IS REGENERATION?

Regeneration varies quite a bit among these creatures. For example, in certain types of worms and in starfish, a tiny part of the body can restore the whole organism. If only a small piece is left, a whole new body will grow!

At the other extreme, we have a kind of regeneration that takes place in our own bodies. The top layer of our skin is constantly being worn off in small bits and replaced by other cells. Our hair and nails are replaced all the time. Even our second set of teeth is a kind of regeneration. And, of course, there is the shedding of feathers and fur and scales among animals, all of which are replaced by a process of regeneration.

The more complicated the organism (and man is a very complicated organism), the less it is able to regenerate. Man, and all mammals, cannot restore an entire organ. But creatures such as salamanders and insects can regenerate a whole limb. What we can regenerate really amounts to repairing damages such as bone fractures, skin and muscle injuries, and some kinds of nerves.

Regeneration takes place in two ways. In one case, new tissue grows from the surface of the wound. In the other, the remaining parts are transformed and reorganized, but new material does not grow.

When new material is grown (such as a limb), it takes place in this way. A regeneration "bud" is formed at the surface of the wound. It is usually cone-shaped and contains an embryonic type of cell, or cells, of the type that were present at the birth of the creature. These cells develop into specialized cells to form the new organ, and as they grow, a new organ is gradually formed!

---

There are many different kinds of baldness, but in most cases, it's a condition over which a man has absolutely no control and for which there simply is no cure.

## WHAT CAUSES BALDNESS?

People say all kinds of things about baldness: It means a man is getting old; or it means he's unusually intelligent; or he's unusually dull. But all baldness really means is that a man is losing his hair!

The kind of baldness we see most often is called pattern baldness. The hair begins to go at the temples, or there's a bald spot at the top of the head, or the baldness appears in some other pattern. This is the most difficult type of baldness to do anything about because it's inherited! The inheritance of pattern baldness is influenced by sex. It appears more in men than in women. Very often the woman carries the gene for this

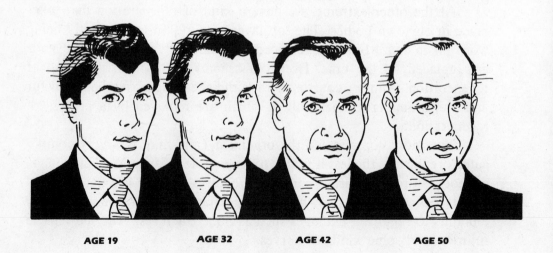

AGE 19          AGE 32          AGE 42          AGE 50

baldness and passes it on to her children. Once this type of baldness appears, about the best thing a man can do is get used to it!

Premature baldness may appear in men as early as the age of twenty-five or even earlier. One cause of this kind of baldness may be a failure to take proper care of the scalp, keep it clean, etc. Sometimes an imbalance of the sex hormones may bring on premature baldness. If proper scalp care is started at once, it may slow up the progress of this type of baldness.

Symptomatic baldness sometimes appears as a sign of infections or other conditions. When health is restored, the hair may grow back again in such cases. Sudden loss of hair can result from typhoid fever, scarlet fever, pneumonia, influenza, and other serious infections.

When there is a gradual loss or thinning of hair, it may sometimes be due to poor nutrition or a disturbance in the glands, especially the pituitary and thyroid glands. And, of course, baldness may come from disorders in the scalp itself, such as scalp injuries or disease.

---

Just as feathers are characteristic of birds, so hair is characteristic of mammals. Why do mammals have hair?— There is a variety of reasons. Let's consider some of them.

## WHY DON'T WOMEN HAVE BEARDS?

The chief value of hair is that it conserves the heat of the body. In the tropics, it may serve an opposite function. Certain tropical animals are protected from direct sunlight by their hair.

Very long hair on certain parts of the body usually serves some special purpose. For instance, a mane may protect an animal's neck from the teeth of its enemies. Tails may act as flyswatters. Crests may attract the opposite sex. In the case of the porcupine, its stiff quills formed of bunched-up hair help it to attack its enemies. Hair may also serve as organs of touch. The whiskers of cats have special nerves that respond quickly to touch.

So you see that hair can serve a different purpose with different mammals. How about human beings? We know that beautiful hair in a woman can be very attractive to men. But we must assume that hair on human beings formerly played a more practical role than it does now.

When an infant is born, he is covered with a fine down. This is soon replaced by the delicate hair which we notice in all children. Then comes the age of puberty, and this coat of hair is transformed into the final coat of hair which the person will have as an adult.

The development of this adult hair coat is regulated by the sex glands. The male sex hormone works in such a way that the beard and the body hair are developed, while the growth of the hair on the head is inhibited, or slowed down in development.

The action of the female sex hormone is exactly the opposite! The growth of the hair on the head is developed, while the growth of the beard and body hair is inhibited. So women don't have beards because various glands and hormones in their bodies deliberately act to prevent this growth.

To explain why this is so, and why men's glands and hormones act to promote growth of beards, we probably have to go back to the early history of man. At one time, the function of the beard was probably to make it easy to tell men and women apart at a distance. It also probably served to give the male an appearance of power and dignity, and so make him more attractive to the female. Nature was helping man to attract the opposite sex, just as she does with other creatures.

---

For men who are becoming a little bald, hair doesn't grow fast enough! But in the case of a young boy, the hair seems to grow too fast!

## HOW FAST DOES HAIR GROW?

The rate at which hair grows has actually been measured and found to be about half an inch a month. The hair doesn't grow at the same rate throughout the day but seems to follow a kind of rhythm.

At night, the hair grows slowly, but as day begins, this is speeded up. Between 10 and 11 AM, the speed of growth is at its greatest. Then the hair grows slowly again. It picks up speed between 4 and 6 PM, and then the growing slows up again. Of course, these variations in the speed of growth are so tiny that you cannot possibly notice them. So don't expect to stand in front of the mirror at 10 AM and be able to watch your hair sprouting up!

If all the hair that grows on the body were to grow in a sort of hair cable, instead of as individual hairs, you would get some idea of the total amount of hair the body produces. This hair cable would grow at the rate of 1.2 inches per minute, and by the end of the year, the tip would be 37 miles away!

Not all people have the same amount of hair. Blond people have finer hair and more hair than dark persons. Red-haired people have the coarsest and the fewest hairs.

---

Most of us have a vague idea that somewhere inside of us there are coils and coils of intestines, amazing passageways through which food passes in the process of digestion. But few people have a clear understanding of just how they work.

## HOW LONG ARE OUR INTESTINES?

The length of the large intestine in animals depends on the kind of food they eat. Meat-eating animals have shorter intestines because there is less digestive work to do. The food they live on has already done part of the job of digestion. People who live on vegetables are supposed to have longer intestines than meat-eating people.

The human intestines are 10 feet long. But when a person dies, the intestines lose their elasticity and stretch to about 28 feet.

Most of the wall of the intestines consists of muscle fibres, so that the intestines can work on the food that goes through them. The intestines mix the food with certain secretions and then pass it along. In order to do this, the small intestine consists of countless loops. Each loop holds a bit of food and works on it, churning it and digesting it for about 30 minutes. Then it passes the food on to the next loop.

To help in this process of digestion, the wall of the small intestine contains about 20,000,000 small glands. These glands send about 5 to 10 quarts of digestive juice into the intestine! This soaks and softens the food so that by the time it goes to the large intestine it's in a semi-liquid state.

If you were to look at the wall of the intestine with a magnifying lens, you would see that it isn't smooth, but resembles velvet. It is covered with millions of tiny tentacle-like villi. The villi tell the glands when to pour out the digestive juice, and also help in the process of digestion themselves.

Food that cannot be digested by juices is digested in the large intestine by bacteria that live there. This is known as putrefaction. Billions of bacteria break down the coarser parts of the food we eat, such as the skins of fruit, and extract valuable materials the body needs.

This is only a rough idea of the way our intestines work. They are among the most amazing organs in our bodies, beautifully organized to do hundreds of things to the food we take in to keep alive.

---

This certainly isn't a pleasant subject, but many people suffer from tapeworm and so there is great curiosity about it. A kind of flatworm, the tapeworm is an intestinal parasite.

## WHAT IS A TAPEWORM?

This means that it lives in the digestive tract of another animal, called the host, and is fed by food which the host has partly digested. The host of the tapeworm is nearly always a backboned animal such as a fish, a dog, or a man. The tapeworm has sucking discs on its head, by means of which it attaches itself to the inside of the intestines. It has no sense organs such as eyes or ears.

The muscles of a tapeworm are almost useless, and its nervous system is primitive. It has no mouth or digestive tract; it absorbs dissolved food through the walls of its body.

There are many species of tapeworms, ranging in length from about 1/25 of an inch to 30 feet! They are of many shapes. They may be unsegmented (undivided), or composed of a chain of segment-like parts. These grow one after the other, always forming behind the head. Each adult is both male and female.

How can a human being get a tapeworm inside his digestive tract? It could happen in the following way: The fertilized eggs of a tapeworm are passed out by the worm. Then a hog eats the eggs. Then the larvae hatch in the hog's intestine.

Inside the hog, these small larvae burrow through the wall of the intestine and go to other parts of the hog's body. When they settle, they form a hard cyst.

Now suppose a human being eats pork that has been improperly cooked. (Proper cooking would kill the larvae in the cyst.) The human digestive juices free the larvae. They then attach themselves to the human intestines and there develop into adults—and a human being finds he has a tapeworm!

The harm a tapeworm does is taking part of the nourishment of the host's food and secreting poisonous substances. Tapeworms do not cause death to man except in rare cases. There are now drugs which can remove a tapeworm from the intestines.

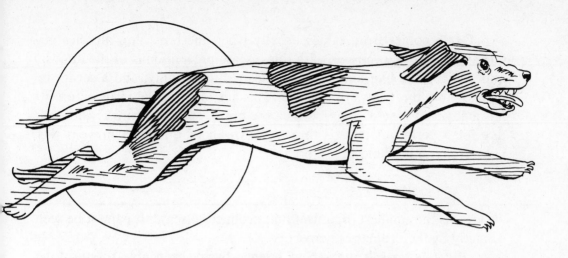

Rabies is one of the oldest diseases known to man. Once the disease appears in man or animals, death is almost certain. There is no cure for it. Just what is this terrible disease?

## WHAT IS RABIES?

Rabies is a disease that infects the brain and spinal cord, which is why it is so harmful to the life of the body. The infection is caused by a virus, which means a germ too small to be seen with the ordinary microscope.

The rabies virus can infect all warm-blooded animals, but man receives it most often when bitten by a dog infected with the virus. This is why when a human being is bitten by a dog, an effort is always made to find the dog and examine it to see if it might have rabies. It just doesn't pay to take chances!

It isn't too easy to tell when a dog has been infected with rabies because it takes such a long time for the disease to show up—usually four to six weeks. At first the dog is quiet, has a fever, and isn't interested in food. Then it becomes excited. Saliva froths from the mouth. It growls and barks, and is likely to bite. After these symptoms appear, it's pretty hopeless. The dog will die in about three to five days.

In human beings, the disease begins much as it does in the dog. A man who is infected by rabies will be quiet at first. He will have fever and feel strange. Soon he feels his muscles draw strongly together. When he tries to drink, the muscles of his mouth and throat tighten, as if he were in a spasm. The muscle spasms are due to changes in the nervous system. But it was believed that they were due to an actual fear of the water, so rabies was given another name—"hydrophobia." This means "fear of water," and is not a true description of the disease.

Death comes from rabies usually when the breathing muscles go into spasm. As you can see, with this disease prevention is of the utmost importance. The bite area must be cleaned thoroughly, and a serum is given within three days of the bite. This acts against the virus before it has a chance to increase and attack the brain. Injections are given each day for a period of two or three weeks. All of this is to prevent the virus from taking hold in the body.

---

A virus is the smallest organism that produces disease. It cannot be seen directly by the ordinary microscope.

But this doesn't mean that science hasn't been able to study the

## CAN A VIRUS BE SEEN?

structure of a virus. Today there are ultramicroscopes that enable these tiny organisms to become visible. And science is able to know quite a bit about the sizes and shapes of various types of viruses by means of the electron microscope.

The electron microscope uses beams of electrons instead of rays of light. The electrons pass through the specimen being observed and strike a photographic plate on which a picture is obtained. In this way, it is possible to magnify an object about 100,000 times.

By using the electron microscope, it has been shown that viruses range in size from about 300 millimicrons to 10 millimicrons. What is a millimicron? It is one thousandth of a micron. And a micron is about one twenty-five thousandth of an inch.

Nobody is quite sure yet exactly what viruses are. Some scientists think they are closely related to bacteria. Other investigators believe they are like elementary particles, similar to "genes." Still others believe viruses are possibly midway between living and nonliving matter.

As far as we know, viruses can grow and reproduce only within living tissue. This means it's impossible to cultivate them away from living tissue, and it makes it difficult to study their growth habits. That's why they are classified by their ability to infect living cells and by the reactions they produce in the body of animals or humans.

Does the virus produce a poison or toxin? It is now believed that they do produce toxins, but the toxin and the virus particle cannot be separated. And we still don't know how these toxins produce disease if they do!

Bacteria are the most widespread creatures in the world. Everything we touch, every breath of air contains millions of them. About 80 per cent of all bacteria are harmless. A small percentage is actually useful to

## WHAT IS AN ANTIBODY?

us, and a small group of them are harmful to human beings.

Since man is constantly taking in bacteria of all kinds, it is obvious that our body and these bacteria form a kind of "working" relationship. Our body supports colonies of bacteria and in turn these bacteria may perform useful functions, such as helping to decompose food.

But what about harmful bacteria which enter our body? For example, the bacteria that cause diphtheria produce a powerful poison called "diphtheria toxin," which spreads through the blood system. Other bacteria, not so deadly, also produce poisons in our blood.

When this happens, our body produces substances to fight these poisons or toxins. These substances are called antibodies. Certain specific antibodies which are produced to fight bacterial toxins are known as antitoxins.

They have the power to nullify any harmful effect produced by the toxin by combining with it. Each antibody is specific for the substance or toxin which causes it to be produced. It's as if the body had a big police force. As soon as a dangerous stranger enters, a policeman meets him and goes along with him to be sure he'll do no harm.

But the body doesn't produce enough antibodies to handle each kind of harmful bacteria that enters our body. Doctors then inject serum containing antitoxin to combat many diseases.

All around us there are invisible forms of life which we call germs. They are in the air, in the soil, in the water we drink and the food we eat. Many of them are harmless or even beneficial to man, but others may

## WHAT IS IMMUNITY?

cause diseases.

The human body has many natural weapons to fight off the attack of the harmful germs. For instance, the digestive juices and the blood itself kill off many kinds of germs. But certain ones enter the body and start an infection. Then the antigerm "soldiers" in the body spring into action. These are the white corpuscles in the blood. They can pass right through the thin walls of blood vessels and they can wander all over the body. The white blood corpuscles gather at the point of attack and destroy the germs by feeding on them.

But disease isn't always caused by a direct attack of germs. Germs throw off a chemical substance called a "toxin" which acts as a poison in the body. Once again, the body has a built-in defense. The toxin causes certain cells in the body to go to work to produce a substance that destroys the toxin. This is called an "antitoxin." If the antitoxin is produced quickly enough and in enough quantity, the germ poison is neutralized. The body gets well.

This antitoxin is always a very special one that works only against the toxin for which it was produced. It remains in the blood for some time after the toxin has disappeared. Now suppose the same germ attacks the body and produces new toxin. Instead of becoming sick, we show no symptoms of the disease at all! The reason is that our body already has a resistance to the disease; it has the antitoxin all ready. We call this condition "acquired" immunity. It is "acquired" because our resistance came after the original attack of the germs.

Now let us suppose there is an attack of germs upon the body, spreading toxins through our system, and yet we don't get that specific disease. This means our blood had enough antitoxin in it to begin with to prevent the specific poison from doing any harm. We call this a "natural" immunity. It is a quality of our blood that we inherited.

If we introduce a little toxin in our blood so it can produce antitoxin to prevent disease, we call it artificial immunity. This is exactly what happens when we are vaccinated against diphtheria and typhoid.

---

The next time you step out of the bath tub or shower, notice the tracks made by your wet feet. If the tracks are kidney-shaped, your foot is normal. If the prints your feet make have the shape of a sole, because the entire sole touches the floor, you have flat feet.

## WHAT CAUSES FLAT FEET?

The foot is a tripod, because it stands on three points. One is the heel in back. The other two are the two supporting points in the ball of the foot. Over these three points the foot forms an arch. This arch is not firm, but is elastic and springy. This is due to the arrangement of the bones, cartilage, ligaments, tendons, and muscles of the foot.

Actually, from an "engineering" point of view, a springy arch is the best type of construction for a structure that has to support weight. The space beneath the arch in the foot is filled with fat. Through this fat go the blood-vessels, nerves, and tendons of the toes, without being squeezed during walking.

When man went about barefoot outdoors, he probably never had any trouble with his feet. The reason is that the irregular and "springy" nature of the earth forces the foot to take a new position with every step. In this way, the entire foot, including the delicate muscles and ligaments of the arch, are always active. This gives all parts of the foot plenty of exercise.

When we walk on smooth city streets and hard floors, only a few points of the foot are constantly stimulated. So the foot adapts itself in a special way to this uniform stimulation. It actually remains in a state known as "spastic tension." This spastic state of the foot disurbs the process whereby all parts of the foot are fed and exercised as they should be. Certain tissues, where the blood circulates poorly, become tired, anemic, and weak. Then the arch of the foot becomes unable to bear the weight of the body and it drops down. The result is flat feet!

Of course, some cases of flat feet are due to the fact that certain people are born with naturally weak tissues. They are just born with weak arches.

---

## WHY DO WE BLINK OUR EYES?

When we drive an automobile in bad weather, it is very important to have the windshield wiper working efficiently. Yet the best windshield wiper ever made for any automobile can't compare to the "windshield wiper" nature has given us for our eyes!

The lids of our eyes, which move up and down when we blink, are our built-in windshield wipers. The lids are made up of folds of skin, and they can be raised and lowered by certain muscles. But they move so rapidly that they don't disturb our vision in any way.

A curious thing about our lids is that they work automatically, just as windshield wipers do on an automobile when they're turned on. We blink our eyes every six seconds! This means that in the course of a lifetime, we pull them back and forth about a quarter of a billion times!

Why is blinking important to us? How does it protect our eyes? One reason has to do with our eyelashes. These are the short curved hairs which are attached to each lid. Their job is to catch dust which might go into our eyes. When you walk through rain or a sandstorm, the lids automatically drop down and the eyelashes keep out foreign matter. The eyebrows, by the way, carry off rain or perspiration to a side, so that the drops won't run into the eyes.

But the chief benefit of blinking is that this provides automatic lubrication and irrigation of the eyes. Along the edge of each lid there are twenty or thirty tiny sebaceous glands. These glands have their opening between the lashes. Every time our lids close, these glands go to work and a secretion comes out. This secretion lubricates the edge of the eye lid and the lashes, so that they won't become dry.

Here is how blinking provides "irrigation" for the eye. In each eye we have a tear gland, where the liquid that makes tears is stored. Every time we blink, the eyelid applies suction to the opening of the tear gland and takes out some of the fluid. This prevents the eye from drying out. We might say that we "cry" every time we blink our eyes!

---

You know what a "cataract" is in nature. It's a great waterfall or down-pouring of water. Now why should a certain kind of eye trouble also be called a "cataract?"

## WHAT IS A CATARACT OF THE EYE?

This is because in ancient times it was believed that this particular eye trouble was caused by an opaque film that came down like a cataract over the lens of the eye. A cataract of the eye is simply a cloudy or opaque discoloration within the lens of the eye. It may or may not interfere with vision. In fact, many people may have cataracts without knowing it.

The way people find out they have cataracts is when parts of the field of vision become blurred or cloudy. Another sign is when such a person can see better in the twilight than when the light is good. When there is less light the pupil is larger and this enables more light to enter the eye.

A cataract causes the pupil of the eye to appear gray or white instead of black. Among old people with cataracts, the pupils may become very small or contracted. When a person has total cataract, the entire lens of the eye becomes milky.

A cataract is generally regarded as a disease of old age. But a baby may have a cataract at birth, or in early childhood. Sometimes people get a cataract of the eye as a result of injury or from circulatory diseases.

When children have cataracts, it is possible to restore useful vision to the eyes by means of a surgical operation without removing the lenses of the eye. But usually when a cataract begins to impair the vision so that a person can't carry on his normal activities, an operation is necessary that will remove the lenses. This is done on one eye at a time to avoid a long period of total blindness.

A great many people who must have such an operation naturally worry about it quite a bit. But the fact is that a good eye surgeon can perform such an operation with very little risk of failure. After about six weeks, the eyes are fitted with glasses which enable the patient to see almost as well as he did with the lenses of his eyes.

Sleeping sickness is a very serious disease that attacks men and animals in Africa.

It is an infection caused by parasites called "trypanosomes." These

## WHAT IS SLEEPING SICKNESS?

parasites, or germs, are carried by the tsetse fly which is common in many parts of central Africa.

The tsetse fly may pick up the parasites when it bites a sick man or animal. The trypanosomes enter the fly's stomach and begin to multiply.

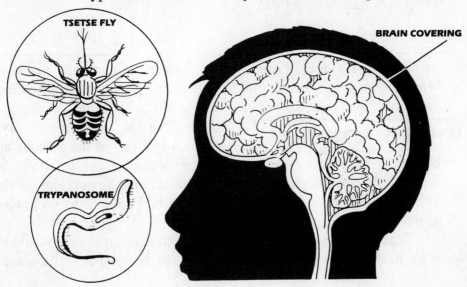

TSETSE FLY

TRYPANOSOME

BRAIN COVERING

They then pass through the salivary glands which supply juice to the fly's mouth. Here they develop into forms which can infect man.

When the fly bites a man, the parasites are injected beneath the skin. A tiny sore spot appears. During the next three weeks trypanosomes begin to circulate in the blood. About this time the infected man begins to have fever that comes and goes. Often, the skin breaks out in a rash. The brain becomes slightly swollen. In some parts of Africa the infection sometimes stops here and the sick man usually recovers.

But in Rhodesia and Nyasaland, the disease takes a more serious form. Within a year, the patient begins to show signs that his brain has become affected. He develops severe headaches. He becomes excited very easily. He begins to act in an uncontrollable way.

Then comes the next stage. He becomes very quiet. And finally, he goes to sleep—and stays asleep. He is in a coma, which means he is unconscious. He still has fever. Finally, he becomes paralyzed, his body wastes away, and he dies.

The reason the person becomes unconscious is that an infection takes place in a very important part of the body—the brain and meninges, which is the covering of the brain. There are many things that may cause an infection, or inflammation, of the brain. Such a condition is called "encephalitis." African sleeping sickness is really a severe form of encephalitis.

By the way, the tsetse fly does not pass on the germ of this disease to its offspring. So sleeping sickness would die out—if there were no sick animals or men for the fly to bite!

---

Asthma is not a disease itself, but a symptom of some other condition. When a person has asthma, he finds it hard to breathe because there is an obstruction to the flow of air into and out of the lungs.

## WHAT IS ASTHMA?

This barrier or obstruction may be caused by a swelling of the mucous membranes, or by a constriction of the tubes leading from the windpipe to the lungs. When a person has an attack of asthma, he develops shortness or breath, wheezing, and coughing. The attack may come on gradually or develop suddenly.

The only way to get rid of asthma is to find out the cause and eliminate it. The cause may be an allergy, an emotional disturbance, or atmospheric conditions. If a person develops asthma before he is 30 years old, it is usually the result of an allergy. He may be sensitive to pollens, dust, animals, or certain foods or medicines.

There are many dusts and pollens which cause asthma. Children, especially, tend to develop asthma from food allergies which may be caused by eggs, milk, or wheat products.

Doctors have also observed that an attack of asthma may be caused by emotional disturbance. For example, if a person has family troubles or financial worries asthma may develop. In many cases the emotional disturbance consists of a feeling of being unwanted or unloved. This produces a state which sets off a chain reaction ending in an attack of asthma.

This is why in cases of asthma the diagnosis by the physician is very important. He will take a complete and careful medical history of the patient. He will ask all kinds of questions about the patient's eating habits, health habits, and environment. If there has been even the slightest change in the person's routine, he will investigate to see if it has anything to do with the attack of asthma. It may have come after a visit to relatives who keep certain animals, or a visit to the beach, or after eating certain new foods. People who have asthma are often put on special diets by the doctor.

---

Every now and then you meet somebody whose nose seems all stuffed up, or he complains of pains in the eyes and cheeks, and headaches. When you ask him if he has a cold, he may answer: "No, I have sinus trouble."

## WHAT ARE THE SINUSES?

What is a sinus, and why do people get "sinus trouble?" Strictly speaking, a sinus is a space filled with blood or with air. But for most people, the expression "sinus trouble" means an infection of one of the cavities connected with the nose.

There are eight or more of these small cavities in the bones of the forehead and face. There are two sinuses in the frontal bones in the forehead. The largest sinuses are in the cheek bones. And there are smaller ones that open into the back and sides of the nose.

All these cavities are lined with mucuous membranes. These membranes are continuations of those in the nose, and the secretions from the sinuses drain through the nose. There are many theories about why we have these sinuses. It may be that they help to warm the nasal passages and to keep them moist. Or, they may give more resonance to the voice, or play some part in the sense of smell. It may be that we have them simply to provide vacant spaces in the skull so it won't be so heavy!

Sinuses may become infected after a severe cold, or influenza, or some other infectious disease. When sinuses are infected, we feel pain in the face, in the forehead, or behind the eyes, which usually comes on about the same time every day. There is sometimes a discharge from the nose.

The pain is caused by the discharge which collects in the sinus and cannot get out because the mucuous membrane which is connected with the nose is swollen. Sometimes the sinus in the cheek bone, called the "antrum," is infected as the result of a dental disease.

An operation for sinus trouble is rarely required. When it is done, the purpose is to enlarge the opening into the nose so that better drainage will take place. The best thing to do about sinus trouble is to prevent it. Great care should be taken to avoid colds. A doctor should be allowed to treat any obstruction in the nose during the early stages, and the dentist should have a chance to treat any dental disease before it becomes serious. Also, it is probably a good idea not to live in hot stuffy rooms, which may help bring on sinus trouble.

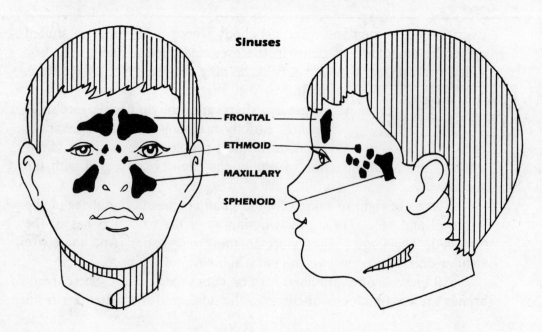

**Sinuses**

**FRONTAL**

**ETHMOID**

**MAXILLARY**

**SPHENOID**

During the "hay fever season," newspapers in many cities publish the day's pollen count. What is pollen, what does it have to do with hay fever, and what is a pollen count?

## WHAT IS A POLLEN COUNT?

A person is said to have hay fever when he is sensitive to pollen and some other substances that are present in the air. Pollen is the reproductive element of plants and is contained in the flowers of most plants. Usually, it occurs as a fine dust or grains.

While insects spread pollen, it is the wind that spreads most of the pollen that causes hay fever. There are three chief groups of plants whose pollen causes hay fever, and each of these groups has a different season. For example, trees produce the pollen that causes hay fever during April and May, various grasses are responsible for hay fever that comes from May to July, and weeds produce the pollen that causes hay fever from August to October.

Since some weeds can produce more than 100,000 pollen grains from a single plant, you can see that at certain times there can be quite a bit of pollen in the air. Naturally, the more pollen there is about, the more the hay fever victims suffer.

This is why a pollen count is taken. People who must leave the area during the heavy pollen season know when to come back. The way a pollen count is taken is quite simple. A glass slide, one side of which is coated with oil, is placed in a horizontal position in the atmosphere to be tested. The slide is usually left for 24 hours. Then the pollen grains collected on it are counted with the aid of a microscope.

Wind and weather have a great deal to do with the amount of pollen in the air. Heavy rains during the summer months cause plants to flourish and produce large quantities of pollen. If the summer months are dry, much smaller amounts of pollen will be produced. Sunshine helps the pollen mature, while damp weather retards it. If it rains in the early part of the day, the spreading of pollen will be held down somewhat.

The reason we call it "hay fever," by the way, is that the symptoms of the disease appeared during the haying season in England. A doctor in 1812 wrote a report on it and called it "hay fever," and the name has remained.

Probably the most complex and difficult musical instrument that can be imagined is the apparatus in human beings that produces speech! In order for sounds and letters to be formed, this entire apparatus must be

## WHY DO PEOPLE STAMMER?

used. This includes the abdomen, chest, larynx, mouth, nose, diaphragm, various muscles, tongue, palate, lips, and teeth!

The most important ones used in making spoken sounds are the muscles of the mouth, the palate, lips, and tongue. The only reason we can "play" this instrument so well, is that we learned how to do it when we were most adaptable during early childhood, and because we have practiced it ever since!

Obviously, if we can't play this instrument (the vocal apparatus) with perfect coordination, then something happens to our speech. It comes out wrong and we stammer.

Stammering, or stuttering, occurs when there is a spasm in one or more of the organs that are involved in producing speech. Our production of words is suddenly checked; there is a pause, and this is often followed by a repetition in quick succession of the sound at which we stopped originally.

There are many grades of stammering. It can range from a slight inability to pronounce certain letters or syllables easily, to a condition in which muscles of the tongue, throat, and face are caught in a spasm.

Stammering rarely shows itself before the age of four or five. A child may begin to stammer because there is actually something wrong with one of the organs used in producing sounds. Very often, an emotional disturbance will cause stammering.

Usually, when a person stammers, it is the "explosive" consonants that give the most trouble . . . "b, p, d, t, k," and the hard "g." An explosive consonant is produced by checking the air on its way out, pressing the lips together, then suddenly stopping the interruption of the air by opening the lips. Try to see how you make the "b" sound. It's explosive!

Stuttering may often be corrected if a person gets instruction in reading and speaking slowly and deliberately, carefully pronouncing each syllable. Of course, if an emotional disturbance is the cause for stammering, special treatment is necessary.

Nobody ever needs an antidote unless he has been poisoned. An antidote by itself has no meaning. It is a substance which prevents the action
of a poison. And a poison is any substance which produces harmful or

## WHAT IS AN ANTIDOTE?

deadly effects on living tissue.
There are basically four kinds
of poisons, divided according to the way they affect the body. Corrosive
poisons (like strong acids) destroy tissues locally. Irritant poisons
produce congestion of the organ with which they come in contact. The
next kind of poison, neurotoxins, affect the nerves within the cell. And
finally, the hemotoxins combine with the blood and prevent oxygen from
forming hemoglobin. Carbon monoxide (such as comes from the ex-
haust of an automobile) is a hemotoxin. It causes death because the
blood is deprived of oxygen that nourishes the tissues and brain.

In treating cases of poisoning, three things are usually done immediately. The first is to dilute the poison. This is done by having the
patient drink as much water as possible. The next step is to empty the
stomach, and this is done by inducing vomiting. Then a specific antidote is given against the particular poison.

Antidotes act in several different ways in preventing the action of
a poison. One way is by combining chemically with the poisonous substance, thus making it harmless. For example, soda combines with
an acid, vinegar combines with lye.

An antidote may also act physically by coating the mucous membranes with a protective layer. Olive oil and milk act as antidotes in this
way. A third way antidotes may work is by absorbing the poisonous
substances on the surface of finely divided particles. Charcoal acts in
this way. Some antidotes actually produce the opposite effect from the
original poison in the body, and so they counteract the action of the
poison. Of course, one of the chief things a doctor tries to do in a case
of poisoning is to eliminate the poison from the body, and there are
many ways to accomplish this.

The best rule to follow is prevention. Poisonous substances should
be kept where children cannot get at them, and products that contain
poison should be clearly marked and carefully stored.

# CHAPTER 4
# HOW THINGS BEGAN

What does the word "superstition" mean to you? When you try to define it, don't you find it's quite hard to do so?

Suppose, for example, you said it was a belief in something that

## HOW DID SUPERSTITIONS BEGIN?

wasn't really so. Well, there are many things all of us believe in that can't be proved. Besides, at certain times in man's history, everyone believed in certain things that we now regard as superstitions. And the people who believed in them at that time weren't superstitious at all!

For example, they believed that the shadow or reflection of a person was a part of the soul. So they considered that you would harm the soul if you broke anything on which this shadow or reflection appeared. Therefore, they considered it harmful or "unlucky" to break a mirror. But remember, at that time this was a belief held by most people.

Today, if someone considers it "unlucky" to break a mirror he is superstitious, because today we no longer believe that a shadow or reflection is part of the soul. So a superstition is actually a belief or practice that people cling to after new knowledge or facts have appeared to disprove them. That's why it's impossible to say when superstition began.

In ancient times man tried to explain events in the world as best he could with the knowledge at hand. He didn't know much about the sun, stars, moon, comets, and so on. So he made up explanations about them and followed certain practices to protect himself from their "influence." That is why astrology was an accepted belief at one time. But with the development of science, the heavenly bodies came to be known and understood. The old beliefs should have died out. When they didn't and when people still believed, for example, that seeing a shooting star brought good luck, then these beliefs became superstitions.

Man has always had superstitions about numbers and about days. Some were supposed to be lucky; some, unlucky. Why the number 13 came to be considered unlucky no one really knows, though there are some

## WHY IS FRIDAY THE 13TH CONSIDERED UNLUCKY?

theories about it. One explanation has to do with Scandinavian mythology. There were 12 demigods, according to this legend, and then Loki appeared, making the 13th. Since Loki was evil and cruel and caused human misfortunes, and since he was the 13th demigod, the number 13 came to be a sign of bad luck.

Some people think the superstition goes back to the fact that there were 13 persons at the Last Supper, and that Judas was the 13th guest! Whatever its origin, the superstition about the number 13 is found in practically every country in Europe and America.

Superstitions about lucky and unlucky days are just as common as those about numbers, and Friday probably has more than any of them centering about it.

In ancient Rome, the sixth day of the week was dedicated to Venus. When the northern nations adopted the Roman method of designating days, they named the sixth day after Frigg or Freya, which was their nearest equivalent to Venus, and hence the name Friday.

The Norsemen actually considered Friday the luckiest day of the week, but the Christians regarded it as the unluckiest. One reason for this is that Christ was crucified on a Friday.

The Mohammedans say that Adam was created on a Friday, and according to legend, Adam and Eve ate the forbidden fruit on a Friday and they died on a Friday.

Superstitious people feel that when you combine the unlucky number 13 with the unlucky day Friday, you've really got an unlucky day!

---

It seems almost a shame to learn the true facts about Santa Claus. We almost hate to discover what's really behind some tradition we especially enjoy because that might spoil it for us.

## HOW DID THE IDEA OF SANTA CLAUS ORIGINATE?

Well, knowing about Christmas and Santa Claus shouldn't spoil anything for you, but only make it more meaningful. Long before Christ was born, people used to celebrate the winter solstice as the birthday of the sun. This time of year was a holiday in many parts of the world before it became the Christmas celebration. That's why some of the customs and traditions of Christmas go back to pagan times.

The custom of giving presents, for example, goes back to the ancient Romans. In the Bible, as you know, the Wise Men brought gifts to Jesus on the 12th day after his birth. And so in some countries, the children receive their presents not on Christmas, but 12 days later.

In some of the northern countries of Europe, the gifts are exchanged almost three weeks before Christmas. The reason for this is that the gifts are supposed to be brought by Saint Nicholas on the eve of his feast day, December 6th.

Saint Nicholas was a bishop of the fourth century who came to be regarded as a special friend of the children. So, in countries like Holland, Belgium, Switzerland and Austria, and in parts of Germany, Saint Nicholas returns every year with gifts for good children.

When the Dutch came to New York, they brought the traditions of Saint Nicholas with them. They called him *San Nicolaas,* and this soon was changed to *Sankt Klaus,* and then Santa Claus. But in this country, we moved the date of his arrival to Christmas Eve, and gradually his red costume, the reindeer, and his home at the North Pole became part of the tradition.

---

No matter how much we like our own country, and our way of government, and the people of our country, we know it isn't perfect. In fact, there never has been a place on earth where everyone who lived there felt it to be perfect.

## WHAT IS UTOPIA?

But many people have often dreamed of living in a perfect place. What would it be like? Well, no one would be poor. But nobody would be rich either. There would be no need to be rich—since everyone would have all the things he needed. Everyone would be happy all the time. There would be very little need for a government, because the people would be considerate of everyone else.

The trouble with such a place is that no one ever really expects to find it. We know it's "too good to be true." Such a place therefore is "nowhere"—and that's exactly what the word "utopia" means. It's made up of two Greek words meaning "not a place"—or nowhere! But the way we use the word "utopia," we mean a perfect place to live.

The word "utopia" was first used by Sir Thomas More, an English writer who lived in the sixteenth century. He published a book in 1516 called *Utopia* in which he described a perfect island country. His book became very popular.

The idea of utopia, however, goes back long before this book. In fact, More got the idea for his book from the famous ancient Greek philosopher Plato, who wrote a book called "The Republic," in which he described what would be a perfect state.

There were also many legends among such people as the Norse, the Celts, and the Arabs, about a perfect place that was supposed to exist somewhere in the Atlantic Ocean. When the exploration of the Western world actually began, most of these legends were no longer believed. But with More's book, "Utopia," it became common for writers to tell of an imaginary place that was perfect. It existed only in their fantasy.

Today, when people describe certain changes they want to make in government or society, these ideas are sometimes called "utopian." This means they fail to recognize defects in human nature that make a perfect place to live practically impossible.

---

Marriage, as a custom, goes back to the very earliest history of man. It has passed through three stages. The first was marriage by capture. Primitive man simply stole the woman he wanted for his wife.

## HOW DID WEDDINGS START?

Then came marriage by contract or purchase. A bride was bought by a man. Finally came the marriage based on mutual love. But even today we still have traces of the first two stages. "Giving the bride away" is a relic of the time when the bride was really sold. The "best man" at weddings today probably goes back to the strong-armed warrior who helped primitive man carry off his captured bride. And the honeymoon itself symbolizes the period during which the bridegroom was forced to hide his captured bride until her kinsmen grew tired of searching for her!

Today we have "weddings" without realizing that this very word goes back to one of the early stages of marriage. Among the Anglo-Saxons, the "wed" was the money, horses, or cattle which the groom gave as security and as a pledge to prove his purchase of the bride from her father.

Of course, when it comes to wedding customs, most of them can be traced back to ancient meanings which have long been forgotten. For example, the "something blue" which brides wear is borrowed from ancient Israel. In those times brides were told to wear a ribband of blue on the borders of their garments because blue was the color of purity, love, and fidelity.

When we ask, Who giveth this woman to this man? we are going back to the times when a bride was actually purchased. It is believed that the custom of having bridesmaids goes back to Roman times when there had to be ten witnesses at the solemn marriage ceremony.

Why do we tie shoes on the back of newlyweds' cars? It is believed that this goes back to the custom of exchanging or giving away of shoes to indicate that authority had been exchanged. So the shoe suggests that now the husband rather than the father has authority over the bride.

---

This custom is not only found all over the world, but it goes back to very ancient times.

The marriage ceremony, like so many other important events in life, is full of symbolism. (This means that we perform certain acts as symbols of things we wish to express, instead of expressing them directly.)

## WHY DO WE THROW RICE AT THE BRIDE AND GROOM?

The use of rice is one of those symbols. It has played a part in

marriage ceremonies for centuries. In certain primitive tribes, for instance, the act of eating rice together was the way people got married. This was probably because eating together symbolized living together, and rice happened to be the local food.

Among other peoples, the bride and groom first ate rice together to be married, and then rice was sprinkled over them.

In some cases, rice was used at weddings not to bring the bride and groom together, but to protect them from evil spirits. It was believed that these spirits always appeared at a marriage, and by throwing rice after the married couple, these evil spirits were fed and kept from doing harm to the newlyweds.

But for most ancient peoples, rice was a symbol of fruitfulness, and the custom of throwing rice at the bride and groom today goes back to that meaning. It means that we are saying, in symbolic form, "May you have many children and an abundance of good things in your future together!"

---

The wearing of a wedding ring is one of the oldest and most universal customs of mankind. The tradition goes back so far that no one can really tell how it first began.

## WHEN WERE WEDDING RINGS FIRST WORN?

The fact that the ring is a circle may be one reason why it began to be used. The circle is a symbol of completeness. In connection with marriage, it represents the rounding out of the life of a person. We can see how a man without a wife, or a woman without a husband, could have been considered incomplete people. When they are married they make a complete unit, which the circle of the ring symbolizes.

Some people believe the wedding ring really started as a bracelet that was placed on women who were captured in primitive times. Gradually the circular bracelet on the arm or leg, which indicated that she was the property of one man in the tribe, was changed to a ring on the finger.

We know also that primitive man believed in magic. He used to weave a cord and tie it around the waist of the woman he wanted. He believed that with this ceremony her spirit entered his body and she was his forever. The wedding ring may have started this way.

The first people who actually used wedding rings in marriage were the Egyptians. In hieroglyphics, which is Egyptian picture-writing, a circle stands for eternity, and the wedding ring was a symbol of a marriage that would last forever. Christians began to use a ring in marriage around the year 900.

Why is the ring worn on the fourth finger of the left hand? The ancient Greeks believed that a certain vein passed from this finger directly to the heart. But probably the real reason is that we use this finger least of all the fingers, so it's more convenient to wear an ornament on it!

---

Years ago there used to a great many popular jokes that began: "Confucius say. . . ." It seems as if everybody knows that Confucius said many wise things.

## WHO WAS CONFUCIUS?

Confucius was one of the greatest moral teachers of all time. He lived in China about five hundred years before Christ. Confucius studied ancient Chinese writings from which he took ideas that to him seemed important to the development of fine character. Then he taught these ideas to the princes and to the students of all classes who flocked to him for instruction. The rules he laid down 2,400 years ago are still held up as ideals.

Confucius' Chinese name was Kung-Fu-tse. At the age of 22, three years after his marriage, Confucius began to teach men how to live happily. His principle rule for happiness, "What you do not wish done to yourself, do not do to others," was much like the Golden Rule.

Confucius held office under many different princes whom he tried to interest in the right moral conduct, the conduct based on love, justice, reverence, wisdom, and sincerity.

One of his teachings, the reverence for parents, had a tremendous effect on China, because it teaches reverence not only while the parents are living but after they are dead. As a form of ancestor worship, it caused China for a long time to look to the past instead of moving forward.

Confucius did not consider himself a god. In fact, he taught nothing about a supreme being or a hereafter. He believed that man was naturally good and could preserve this goodness by living harmoniously with his fellow men.

Within five hundred years after his death, his teachings became the philosophy of the state. But when Buddhism appeared, the teachings of Confucius were almost forgotten for a period. They were later revived, and even today his teachings influence the lives of millions of people.

---

We think of our way of life as the only one, and when we learn about other civilizations, we are often shocked, or at least surprised. When we mourn somebody, we naturally wear black. What else could one wear?

## WHY IS BLACK WORN FOR MOURNING?

Well, in Japan and China, they wear pure white when mourning! And in some sections of Africa, the natives apply red paint to their bodies as a sign of mourning.

The reason we wear black is simply that, according to our traditions, this is the best way to express grief. When we see people dressed in black mourning clothes they look somber and sad, so it seems natural to us that black is the color of mourning clothes.

But have you ever wondered why we wear mourning clothes at all? Of course, we now do it as a mark of love or respect for someone who has died. But in trying to trace mourning clothes back to their beginnings, scholars have come up with interesting answers.

When we put on mourning clothes, they are usually the reverse of the kind of clothes we wear every day. In other words, it's a kind of disguise. Some people think that ancient peoples put on this disguise because they were afraid that the spirit which had brought death would return and find them!

Now, this might seem pretty far-fetched, if there weren't some peoples who do exactly this even today. Among many primitive tribes in various parts of the world, as soon as someone dies, the widow and other relatives put on all sorts of disguises. Sometimes they cover the body with mud and put on a costume of grass. In other tribes, the women cover their bodies entirely with veils.

So perhaps our black mourning clothes go back to the idea of frightening away spirits or hiding from them! There are other mourning customs that are linked to this fear of spirits. For example, mourning is a period of retirement. We withdraw from normal activities and life.

There are countless examples of primitive and ancient peoples who retired from social life when a relative died. In some cases, the widow spent the rest of her life in a kind of retirement. And it may all have started from the fear of "contaminating" other people with the spirit of death!

---

The Taj Mahal is a love story, a sad and beautiful one. If it didn't exist, we could easily imagine that the story of its construction was simply a fairy tale.

## WHAT IS THE TAJ MAHAL?

Three hundred years ago, there lived in India an emperor called Shah Jahan. His favorite wife was a beautiful and intelligent woman whom he loved greatly and made his counselor and constant companion. Her title was Mumtazi Mahal; its shortened form, Taj Mahal, means "pride of the palace."

In the year 1630 this beloved wife of the emperor died. He was so brokenhearted that he thought of giving up his throne. He decided, out of love for his wife, to build her the most beautiful tomb that had ever been seen.

He summoned the best artists and architects from India, Turkey, Persia, and Arabia, and finally, the design was completed. It took more than twenty thousand men working over a period of 18 years to build the Taj Mahal, one of the most beautiful buildings in the world.

The building itself stands on a marble platform 313 feet square

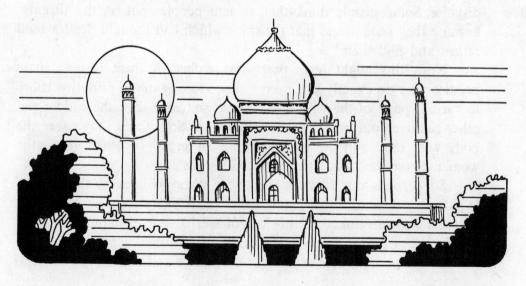

and 22 feet high. Minarets, or towers, rise from each of the four corners. The Taj itself soars another 200 feet into the air. It is an eight-sided building made of white marble, and inlaid with twelve kinds of semi-precious stones in floral designs as well as with black marble inscriptions from the Koran. (The emperor was of the Moslem faith.) The building materials came from many countries, including Arabia, Egypt, Tibet, and various parts of India.

The emperor planned to build an identical tomb of black marble for himself on the other side of the river connected by a silver bridge. But his son imprisoned him in the palace before he could finish, and for the rest of his life, he could only gaze across the river at the shrine of his beloved.

---

No one knows exactly how old the pyramids are. A thousand years before Christ, they were already old and mysterious. The Great Pyramid at Giza has been attributed to King Cheops of the fourth dynasty (about 2900 B.C.).

## HOW WERE THE EGYPTIAN PYRAMIDS BUILT?

The pyramids are tombs. The ancient Egyptian kings believed that their future lives depended upon the perfect preservation of their bodies. The dead were therefore embalmed, and the mummies were hidden below the level of the ground in the interior of these great masses of stone. Even the inner passages were blocked and concealed from possible robbers. Food and other necessities were put in the tombs for the kings to eat in their future lives.

The building of such a tremendous structure was a marvelous engineering feat. It is said that it took 100,000 men working for twenty years to build the Great Pyramid! Each block of stone is 7 feet high. Some are 18 feet across! Let's see if we can trace the story of the building of this particular pyramid.

The blocks of limestone and granite used in building the pyramid were brought by boat from quarries across the Nile and to the south. This could be done for only three months each spring when the Nile was flooded. So it took twenty years and some 500,000 trips to bring all the stone needed!

Boats unloaded at a landing space connected to the site of the pyramid by a stone road. The blocks, weighing about 2 tons each, were then pulled up the road on sledges by gangs of men. Stone blocks pulled up the road were laid out in neat rows and then pulled to the site by other gangs of men. The number of blocks in the Great Pyramid have been estimated at 2,300,000.

As the pyramid rose, a huge ramp was built to get the materials to higher levels. Gangs of men pulled the blocks up the ramp. Each layer of the pyramid was made of blocks of limestone set side by side. Mortar was used to slide the stones, rather than to cement them together. Blocks in the center were rough, but those on the outside were cut more carefully. The final surface was made of very smooth limestone with almost invisible joints. The pyramid has three inside chambers with connecting passages.

---

The history of man is full of cruelty towards those whose sickness we have been unable to understand. For thousands of years, for example, deaf-mutes were treated as if they were dangerous to society. In many

## WHO INVENTED SIGN LANGUAGE?

countries they were regarded as idiots and were locked up in asylums. Very often they were killed to get them out of the way.

In the sixteenth century a man came along who wanted to do something to help the deaf-mutes. He was an Italian doctor named Jerome Cardan who believed that deaf-mutes could be taught by using written characters. His work attracted great interest, and by the seventeenth century, a finger alphabet was worked out which was similar to the finger alphabet in use today. It took another hundred years, however, before the first public school for deaf-mutes was established at Leipzig, Germany. Today, every civilized country in the world has institutions for educating its deaf and hard-of-hearing.

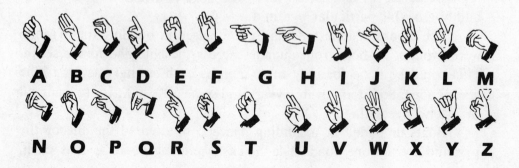

A B C D E F G H I J K L M
N O P Q R S T U V W X Y Z

Most people call a person who has lost any of his sense of hearing deaf. Actually, this term should be used only for those who were born without hearing or who lost their hearing before they learned to talk. Loss of hearing is caused in many ways. It may come about through some disease, or through severe injury to the head, or through something being wrong with the inner ear.

Why can't deaf people talk? Nearly always, it's because the deaf person never heard spoken words! It is a condition that can be remedied. In fact, nearly all deaf children with normal intelligence can learn to talk if they are given special instruction.

Up to about seventy-five years ago, the deaf were taught to communicate ideas almost entirely by means of signs, facial expression, and the finger alphabet. With the hand alphabet, some deaf-mutes can spell out words at the rate of 130 a minute! But they still depend mostly on sign language. For example, the forefinger rubbed across the lips means, "You are not telling me the truth." A tap on the chin with three fingers means, "My uncle."

Today, the deaf are taught to understand what is said to them and even to speak themselves. They learn to speak by watching the lips of the speaker, and by observing and feeling the lips and vocal organs of the teacher and then imitating the motions.

---

If you were unfortunate enough to be blind, one of the greatest losses you would feel would be not being able to read. Just think how important the ability to read books is to you. Well, people realized this a long time ago and tried to find methods for

## WHAT IS THE BRAILLE SYSTEM?

enabling blind people to read.

For example, as far back as 1517 there was a system of engraving letters on blocks of wood so blind people could make them out with their fingers. A person's fingertips are very sensitive, and a blind person can "read" with his fingers. A great many other systems were worked out over the years, using raised lines for the letters. But they all presented one big problem: while blind people could learn to read in this way, they couldn't easily write this way because they couldn't see how to form the letters.

In 1829 a man called Louis Braille, who was blind himself and was a teacher of the blind, developed a system that could be read by the

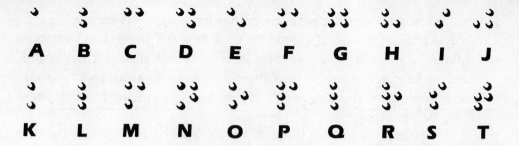

A B C D E F G H I J

K L M N O P Q R S T

blind and written by them too with a simple instrument.

The Braille system consists of dots. Imagine an oblong block. This is called "the Braille cell." On this block are arranged raised dots, from one to six. The cell is 3 dots high and two dots wide. The Braille alphabet consists of different arrangements of the dots. Since 63 combinations are possible, there can be an entire alphabet plus signs for punctuation and contractions and so on. For example, "A" in the Braille system consists of one dot on the upper row at the left. "B" is two dots, in the two upper rows at the left. (Remember, there are three horizontal rows of two dots each.)

The Braille system is one of the most widely used alphabets for the blind, and has helped many blind people to enjoy the pleasures of reading and writing. In fact, today there are about a hundred Braille magazines and newspapers published. Another help for the blind today is the "Talking Book." This is a long-playing record of a book, and there are even special "Talking Books" for blind children.

---

The word "hieroglyphs" means "sacred carvings." Actually, it is not an accurate name for the ancient writing of the Egyptians. It came about because when the early Greeks first saw these writings, they believed they were made by priests for sacred purposes.

## WHAT IS HIEROGLYPHIC WRITING?

But Egyptian hieroglyphics is really one of the oldest known systems of writing. Some of the inscriptions go back to before 3000 B.C., and hieroglyphics continued to be the written language of Egypt for more than 3000 years.

At first the Egyptians used a crude form of picture writing, such as has been used by primitive races throughout the world. The hieroglyphics were simply pictures, each one representing a natural object.

The sun was represented by a disk, the moon by a crescent, water by wavy lines, a man by the figure of a man, and so on.

But these "picturegrams" could not represent the things that the eye could not see—such as thoughts, light, and day. So hieroglyphics in time became symbols of ideas rather than pictures of objects. A disk might suggest "day" instead of only the sun; another symbol meant "turn." These idea signs were called "ideograms."

The next step in the development of hieroglyphics was in the use of images to represent sounds instead of the actual objects. For example, the bee might mean, not an insect, but the syllable "bee." A leaf might represent the syllable "leaf." By putting these together, they would make the word "belief." (We are using English words to show how it was done.) Such hieroglyphics used as sound signs, are known as "phonograms."

Now the Egyptians could write down any words they knew, whether the word meant a thing of which they could draw a picture or not. From these phonograms there developed a series of signs, each representing only a letter. In writing, the Egyptians used only consonants. For example, "drink" would be written "drnk" (using Egyptian words, of course). The Egyptians also kept on using old signs in their writing—ideograms, phonograms, and picturegrams all combined. In time, it became so complicated that the common people couldn't understand it!

---

## WHAT IS CRYPTOGRAPHY?

Suppose you and your friends wanted to set up a system of sending secret messages to each other. You might say, "Instead of using letters, let's use numbers." Each number will stand for a certain letter of the alphabet.

You would then have a code. Cryptography is writing using a secret code. Sometimes the word "cipher" is used instead of code. Did you know that Julius Caesar used a cipher to keep his message secret from enemy eyes? In modern times, ciphers and codes are used by both government and business for important and secret messages.

In general, there are two kinds of cipher. One kind is the substitution of a number, letter, or other symbol for each letter in a message. The other kind is the transposition or rearrangement of the order of the letters in a message.

There are endless ways in which these two types can be used. The first type is the simpler system and is the one boys and girls usually use in a homemade cipher. The word "code" is usually used for a message which can be translated by use of a codebook held by both the sender and the receiver of the message.

Codes and ciphers can be "broken," or solved, by direct methods of deciphering and decoding. To do this, the key to a cipher or codebook is necessary. These are sometimes hard to find.

A scientific method of reading cryptograms (secret messages) has been developed and is called crypto-analysis. A person reading cryptograms usually must determine what language the secret message uses. He must decide whether the message is in cipher or code. Tables of the frequency of the use of letters in a language, and many other things, are necessary in breaking ciphers and codes.

---

## WHO PUBLISHED THE FIRST NEWSPAPER?

The first newspapers were nothing like our papers today. They were more like letters containing news. In the fifth century B.C., there were men in Rome who wrote these newsletters and sent them to people who lived far away from the capital. Something more like our papers was established by Julius Caesar in 60 B.C. He had the government publish a daily bulletin for posting in the Forum. Devoted chiefly to government announcements, it was called *Acta Diurna*, which meant "Daily Happenings."

One of the chief needs for getting news quickly in early days was for business purposes. Businessmen had to know what important things had happened. So one of the first newspapers, or newsletters, was started in the sixteenth century by the Fuggers, a famous German family of international bankers. They actually established a system for gathering the news so that it would be reliable.

In Venice, at about the same time, people paid a fee of one *gazeta* to read notices that were issued by the government every day. These were called *Notizie Scritte* ("Written News").

The first regular newspaper established in London was the *Intelligencer* in 1663. Most early papers that were established could be published only once a week, because both communication and production were slow.

The first American newspaper, *Publick Occurrences,* was started in Boston in 1690, but the governor of the colony quickly stopped it. Benjamin Franklin conducted the *Pennsylvania Gazette* from 1729 to 1765. The people were so eager to have newspapers that by the time of the American Revolution there were 37 of them being published in the Colonies!

One of the most influential newspapers ever published is the *London Times,* which began to be published in 1785 as the *Daily Universal Register.*

---

Every year, when the Nobel Prizes are announced there is a great deal of publicity about the winners. They are interviewed and articles are written about them. This is because winning the Nobel Prize is consid-

## WHAT IS THE NOBEL PRIZE?

ered by most people the highest honor that can be achieved in certain particular fields of work such as chemistry, physics, medicine, and literature. There is also a Nobel Peace Prize, awarded for efforts on behalf of peace.

The curious thing about these prizes is that they were started by a man who did a great deal to help the science of destruction! Alfred Nobel was born in Stockholm and lived from 1833 to 1896. Among the things which he invented and patented were dynamite, blasting gelatin (more powerful than dynamite), and a new kind of detonator for explosives.

It may be that having created such deadly explosives, Nobel felt a need to do something "noble" for the world. He was interested in establishing peace, and had a plan he thought would prevent war. By the way, besides being a brilliant scientist, Nobel was also a poet. He thought that literature and science were the most important factors in human progress.

When he died, Nobel left a fund of $9,000,000. The money was to be used in giving prizes to those who made outstanding contributions in physics, chemistry, medicine, literature, and the advancement of world peace. The prizes averaged about $40,000 each, and were first awarded on December 10, 1901, the anniversary of Nobel's death.

Since Nobel was a Swede, the Nobel Foundation of Sweden distributed the awards. The organizations selected to determine the winners were: for physics and chemistry, the Royal Academy of Science in Stockholm; for medicine, the Caroline Institute of Stockholm; for literature, the Swedish Academy of Literature; for peace, a committee of five persons chosen by the Norwegian Parliament.

Many great people have won Nobel Prizes: among them are Theodore Roosevelt, Albert Einstein, George Bernard Shaw, Marie Curie, Rudyard Kipling, Ernest Hemingway, and Ralph Bunche.

---

Was there actually a Mother Goose who wrote the delightful fairy tales and nursery jingles that all children love? Three different countries give three different answers as to who Mother Goose was.

## WHO WROTE MOTHER GOOSE?

In England, it was believed that Mother Goose was an old woman who sold flowers on the streets of Oxford. In France, there are people who believe that Mother Goose was really Queen Bertha. She married her cousin, Robert the Pious. Because he already had a wife, Queen Bertha was punished by the pope. One of her feet became shaped like that of a goose. From then on, she was called Mother Goose.

In the United States, there are some who say that Mother Goose's name was Elizabeth Fergoose. She was the mother-in-law of a Boston printer who lived in the early part of the eighteenth century.

The first time the tales attributed to Mother Goose were set down was in 1696. For many centuries they had been handed down from

generation to generation by word of mouth. But in that year, a Frenchman called Charles Perrault wrote them down. His collection included *Cinderella* and *Sleeping Beauty*.

Perrault sent the manuscript to a bookseller named Moetjens who lived at The Hague, in Holland. Moetjens published the tales in his magazine in 1696 and 1697. They immediately became popular. In 1697 a printer in Paris published eight of the tales in book form. The volume was called *Histories or Stories of Past Time*. On the cover was a little sign on which was written "Tales of My Mother Goose."

So you see these tales and nursery rhymes have been told and read to children for hundreds of years. The earliest translation of the Mother Goose tales into English was in 1729.

We still don't know who first wrote *Simple Simon, Little Miss Muffet,* and all the others which became part of Mother Goose. But in 1760 a collection of Mother Goose jingles was published in London, and about twenty-five years later it was reprinted and published in Worcester, Massachusetts.

---

Did you ever walk in a forest and suddenly come upon a little brook bubbling merrily along its path? Didn't it sound like music? When the rain pitter-patters against a roof, or a bird sings heartily—aren't these

## HOW DID MUSIC BEGIN?

like music?

When man first began to notice his surroundings, there was a kind of music already here. And then when he wanted to express great joy, when he wanted to jump and shout and somehow express what he felt, he felt music in his being, perhaps before he was able to express it.

Eventually, man learned to sing, and this was the first man-made music. What do you think would be the first thing man would want to express in song? Happiness? Yes, the happiness of love. The first songs ever sung were love songs. On the other hand, when man was face to face with death which brought him fear, he expressed this, too, in a different kind of song, a kind of dirge or chant. So love songs and dirges were the first music man ever made!

Another kind of music came with the development of the dance. Man needed some sort of accompaniment while he danced. So he clapped his hands, cracked his fingers, or stamped on the earth—or beat upon a drum!

The drum is probably one of the oldest instruments man invented to produce sound. It's so old that we can never trace its beginnings, but we find it among all ancient peoples everywhere in the world.

The earliest wind instruments created by man were the whistle and the reed pipe. The whistles were made of bone, wood, and clay. From them, the flute was developed. The flute is so ancient that the Egyptians had it more than 6,000 years ago!

Stringed instruments probably came soon afterward. Did you know that the ancient Egyptians had them, too?

---

Man has always loved to be entertained. From the very beginning of civilization there have been jugglers, acrobats, animal trainers and clowns to entertain people. In ancient Greece there were chariot races,

## HOW DID THE CIRCUS BEGIN?

in China there were contortionists, and in Egypt there were trainers of wild animals.

But it was the Romans who first had the idea of combining such acts and other events into a circus. Actually, the word "circus" comes from the Latin pertaining to races rather than to a type of show. So the circus started with races, and the structures built by the Romans for these races were called circuses. The Circus Maximus was the first and largest of these. It was started in the third century B.C. and was enlarged until it could seat more than 150,000 people!

When the Romans came to these circuses, it was much like arriving at a modern circus or fair grounds. There were vendors of pastry, wine (like our soft drink sellers), and various other merchandise. Admission was free, because the government used these circuses as a way of keeping the masses content.

Meanwhile, in Rome there were all sorts of other entertainment going on which eventually became part of what we call the circus. Some theatres had jugglers, acrobats, ropewalkers and animal trainers. Some of them even had boxing bears! And at the race courses, they had people performing such tricks as riding two horses at once, riders jumping from one running horse to another, and riders jumping their teams over chariots, all of which we have in the modern circus.

During the Middle Ages there was no organized circus as such, but troupes of performers would wander about doing various acts. The first circus, as we know it today, was organized by an Englishman,

Philip Astley, in 1768. He set up a building in London with a number of seats and a ring. He did trick riding on horses and had acrobats, clowns, and ropewalkers. After him, a great many other people had the same idea, and the circus became a popular entertainment all over the world.

---

There are many kinds of puppets, as you know. There are hand puppets, rod puppets, shadow figures, and marionettes. They are little figures operated by strings and wires from above, by rods, or by hands from below.

## WHEN DID PUPPET SHOWS START?

Puppets are as old as the theater itself. The first puppets were probably made in India or Egypt. Puppet theaters thousands of years old have been found in both of these countries. Marionettes, which are puppets animated by strings from above, got their name in Italy. During the early Christmas celebrations, small, jointed nativity figures including the Christ Child and the Virgin Mary were made to move by strings. This kind of puppet became known as a marionette, or little Mary.

In China, Japan, and Java puppet showmen have made figures to represent the heroes, gods, and animals of their legends and stories. In Java, Siam, and Greece they developed shadow-plays. They were made by moving cut-out figures against a vertical sheet lighted from behind. Did you know that special operas for puppets have been written by great composers like Mozart, Haydn, and Gluck?

One of the best-loved of all children's stories tells of the adventures of Pinocchio, a puppet who came to life. You will find many of the same puppet characters famous in different lands. Punch, the famous English puppet, is known in Italy as Punchinello and in France as Polichinelle.

Puppet shows are a way to tell a story or express an idea. They are not hampered by the limitations of live actors. For instance, if you want a character to have a very long nose or big hands, or very short legs, or even wings, a puppet can have them without any trouble at all.

Puppets can also be any size needed. There are some marionettes that are only 6 inches tall, and some have been made 30 or 40 feet tall! Also, it is possible to make puppet animals and they can be just as good actors as people!

---

Probably the greatest honor that could come to an athlete is to win the gold medal at the Olympic Games. But did you know that the idea of having Olympic Games is more than 2,500 years old?

# WHEN DID THE OLYMPIC GAMES START?

According to Greek legend, the Olympic Games were started by Hercules, son of Zeus. The first records we have are of games held in 776 B.C. on the plain of Olympia. They were held every four years for more than 1,000 years, until the Romans abolished them in 394 A.D.

The ancient Greeks considered the games so important that they measured time by the interval between them. The four years were called an Olympiad. The games were an example of the Greek ideal that the body, as well as the mind and spirit, should be developed. Nothing was allowed to interfere with holding the games; if a war happened to be going on, the war was stopped!

Fifteen hundred years later a Frenchman named Baron Pierre de Coubertin had the idea of reviving the Olympic Games. In 1894, following his suggestion, an International Congress of fifteen nations was held in Paris. This Congress unanimously agreed to revive the games and to hold them every four years. Two years later, in the rebuilt stadium at Athens, Greece, the first of the modern Olympic Games was held.

The games today include many sports that didn't even exist in ancient times, such as basketball, water polo, soccer, cycling, shooting, and field hockey.

The modern Olympics are governed by an International Olympic Committee, and each nation has its own National Olympic Committee which is responsible for its country's participation in the Olympics.

---

All kinds of claims have been made about the invention of playing cards. Some people think they originated with the Egyptians, others give the credit to the Arabs, or Hindus, or Chinese.

## HOW DID PLAYING CARDS GET THEIR NAMES?

We do know that playing cards were first used for foretelling the future and were linked with religious symbols. Ancient Hindu cards, for example, had ten suits representing the ten incarnations of Vishnu, the Hindu god.

Playing cards were probably introduced into Europe during the thirteenth century. We can trace the playing cards we have today to certain cards that existed in Italy. They were called "tarots," or picture cards, and there were 22 of them. They were used for fortunetelling or simple games.

These 22 picture cards were then combined with 56 number cards to make a deck of 78 cards. One of the tarot cards was called "il matto," the fool, from which we get our joker. There were four suits in this deck,

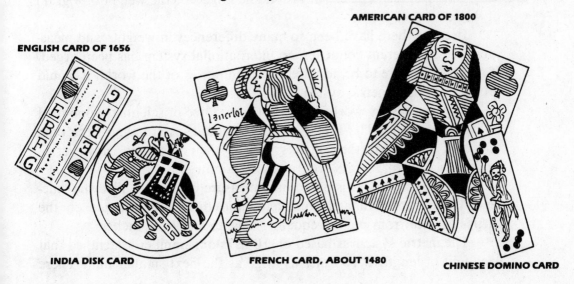

ENGLISH CARD OF 1656

AMERICAN CARD OF 1800

INDIA DISK CARD

FRENCH CARD, ABOUT 1480

CHINESE DOMINO CARD

representing the chalice, the sword, money, and the baton. There were also four "court" cards, the king, queen, knight, and knave.

From these 56 cards of the Italian deck came the 52-card French deck. The French kept the king, queen, knave, and ten numeral cards in each of the four suits, which they gave new names — spade, heart, diamond, and club. The English adopted this deck, which is the deck we now use.

The earliest European cards were hand-painted, and too expensive for general use. With the invention of printing, it became possible for most people to own playing cards.

Early cards were either square, extremely oblong, or even round, but today they are the standard size of 3½ inches by 2½ or 2¼. Many efforts have been made to put the pictures of national heros or current events on cards, but these usually end up as novelties. The figures on American and English cards wear costumes from the time of Henry VII and Henry VIII.

---

In deciding upon a unit of measurement, it is possible to pick anything. For example, the average height of a man could possibly have been a unit of measurement. In fact, some of the units used today in English-

## WHAT IS THE METRIC SYSTEM?

speaking countries are based on such things as the distance from a man's elbow to the tip of his middle finger, or the weight of a grain of wheat.

Because there have been so many differences in weights and measures used in different countries, an international system has been urged. If one system were to be adopted by all countries of the world, it would probably be the metric system.

This is a system worked out by a committee of scientists appointed in France in 1789. The English-speaking countries are almost the only ones that do not use the metric system in their measures. However, it is used in scientific work even in those countries.

The metric system is based on a measure of length called the "meter." This is approximately one ten-millionth of the distance on the earth's surface from pole to equator. It is about 39.37 inches.

The metric system is based on 10 as is our number system, so that each unit of length is 10 times as large as the next smaller unit. There are square and cubic units for measuring area and volume which correspond to the units of length.

The unit of weight is the gram, which is the weight of a cubic centimeter of pure water. The liter is a measure used as the quart is used, but it is a little larger, The hectare, which is 10,000 square meters, is used as the acre is used, but is 2.471 acres. The metric system is more convenient to use than the English system because its plan is the same as that of our number system.

Here are some equivalents for the metric and English systems: one foot equals .305 meter; one inch equals 2.540 centimeters; one mile equals 1.609 kilometers; one quart (liquid) equals .946 liter.

---

Perhaps you didn't realize that the zero had to be invented! Actually one of man's greatest inventions, it was a concept that has had a tremendous influence on the history of mankind because it made the development of higher mathematics possible.

## WHO INVENTED THE ZERO?

Up until about the sixteenth century, the number system used in Europe was the Roman system, invented about two thousand years ago. The Roman system was not a simple one. It is built on a base of 10. Thus the mark "X" means 10. The letter "C" means 100. The letter "M" stands for 1,000. The mark for 1 is "I," for 5 "V," for 50 "L," and for 500 "D." 4 is shown by "IV," or 1 less than 5. To indicate 1,648, you write: "MDCLXLVIII." In the Roman system, to read the number, sometimes you count, sometimes you subtract, sometimes you add.

Long before the birth of Christ, the Hindus in India had invented a far better number system. It was brought to Europe about the year 900 by Arab traders and is called the Hindu-Arabic system.

In the Hindu-Arabic system, all numbers are written with the nine digits — 1, 2, 3, 4, 5, 6, 7, 8, 9 — and the zero, 0. In a number written with this system each figure has a value according to the place in which it is written.

We know the number 10 means 1 ten, because the "1" is written in the 10's place and the zero shows there are no units to be written in the unit place. The number 40 means four 10's and no units, or 40 units. The zero shows that the 4 is written in the 10's place.

The Romans had no zero in their system. To write 205, they wrote

"CCV." They had no plan using place values. In the Hindu-Arabic system we write 205 by putting 2 in the 100's place to show 200, 0 in the 10's place to show that there are no 10's, and the 5 in the 1's place to show that there are 5 units.

---

In many doctors' offices, you will see a framed document on the wall called the Hippocratic Oath. This is an oath taken by doctors when they graduate from medical school. What is this oath and who was Hippocrates?

## WHO WAS HIPPOCRATES?

Before the age of scientific medicine, which we have today, man had a form of medicine that depended on magicians and witch doctors. Then, in ancient Egypt and India, a more sensible form of medicine developed. The ancient Egyptians, for example, were good observers. They had medical schools, and practiced surgery. But the treatment of disease was still a part of the Egyptian religion, with prayers, charms, and sacrifices as a part of the treatment.

Scientific medicine had its beginning in Greece when a group of men who were not priests became physicians. The most famous of these, Hippocrates, who lived about 400 B.C., is called "the father of medicine."

His approach to medicine was scientific. He put aside all superstition, magic, and charms. He and his pupils made careful records of their cases. Some of their observations are considered to be true even today: Weariness without cause indicates disease. When sleep puts an end to delirium, it is a good sign. If pain is felt in any part of the body, and no cause can be found, there is mental disorder.

Hippocrates also had strong ideas about what a doctor should be and how he should behave. This is incorporated in his Hippocratic Oath, which among many others contains such ideas as the following:

"I will follow that system of regimen which according to my ability and judgment I consider for the benefit of my patients, and abstain from whatever is deleterious and mischievous. I will give no deadly medicine to anyone if asked, nor suggest any such counsel . . . Whatever, in connection with my professional practice or not in connection with it, I see or hear in the life of men which ought not to be spoken of abroad, I will not divulge, as reckoning that all such should be kept secret."

148

The problem of caring for the weak and sick members of society has existed from the very earliest times. But the idea of hospitals is a new one in the history of man.

## HOW DID HOSPITALS BEGIN?

The Greeks, for instance, had no public institutions for the sick. Some of their doctors maintained surgeries where they could carry on their work, but they were very small, and only one patient could be treated at a time. The Romans, in time of war, established infirmaries, which were used to treat sick and injured soldiers. Later on, infirmaries were founded in the larger cities and were supported out of public funds.

In a way, the Roman influence was responsible for the establishment of hospitals. As Christianity grew, the care of the sick became the duty of the Church. During the Middle Ages monasteries and convents provided most of the hospitals. Monks and nuns were the nurses.

The custom of making pilgrimages to religious shrines also helped advance the idea of hospitals. These pilgrimages were often long, and the travelers had to stop overnight at small inns along the road. These inns were called *hospitalia,* or guest houses, from the Latin word *hospes,* meaning "a guest." The inns connected with the monasteries devoted themselves to caring for travelers who were ill or lame or weary. In this way the name "hospital" became connected with caring for the afflicted!

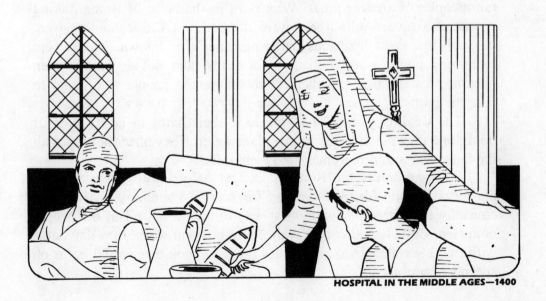

**HOSPITAL IN THE MIDDLE AGES—1400**

Since living conditions during the Middle Ages were not very comfortable or hygienic, the hospitals of those days were far from being clean or orderly. In fact, many a hospital would put two or more patients in the same bed!

During the seventeenth century, there was a general improvement in living conditions. People began to feel that it was the duty of the state to care for its ailing citizens. But it wasn't until the eighteenth century that public hospitals became general in the larger towns of England. Soon, the idea of public hospitals began to spread, and they appeared all over Europe.

In North America, the first hospital was built by Cortes in Mexico City in 1524. Among the British colonies, the first hospital was established by the East India Company on Manhattan Island in 1663.

---

## WHEN DID PEOPLE START USING BATHTUBS?

We feel very proud in this country about our national cleanliness. Doesn't every home have a bathtub? Well, did you know that at one time there were more homes with radios in this country than with bathtubs?

In spite of all our pride concerning cleanliness, we have never made as big a fuss about bathing and baths as have certain peoples of ancient times! Why right in the heart of Rome, taking up about a square mile, there were the baths of Caracalla that were probably the most luxurious baths man has ever known. There were swimming pools, warm baths, steam baths, and hot-air baths — even libraries, restaurants, and theaters to amuse the people who came to take the baths!

The wealthy classes of Rome took their baths in costly tubs or pools, and they didn't bathe in just plain water. They filled the tubs with the finest wines and perfumes, and even milk!

But long before the Romans, in fact before history was written, man was bathing for pleasure and for health. Swimming in rivers, of course, was always the commonest way to take a bath. But the people of ancient Crete had already advanced to the point where they had baths with running water. In ancient times the Jews took ceremonial baths on special occasions.

By the third century B.C., almost every large Greek city had at least one public bath. By this time, too, the wealthy classes had private baths and pools in their homes.

During the Dark Ages people must have looked rather dark and dirty. They just weren't much concerned about keeping clean. When the Crusaders invaded Palestine they were surprised to find that it was part of the Mohammedan religion to bathe at certain times of the day, before praying.

They tried to introduce regular bathing into Europe when they came back, but they didn't have much success. In fact, it wasn't until about 100 years ago that people began to understand the importance of bathing regularly!

---

When you see a man with a beard, doesn't he somehow look dignified, or even important? In the history of man, this has been the usual attitude towards beards. It was a sign of manhood.

## WHEN DID MEN BEGIN SHAVING THEIR BEARDS?

That's why you will find that in ancient times, when an important person was shown, he was usually shown with a beard. The Greek god, Zeus, was shown with a beard; drawings representing God showed a beard; Abraham, King Arthur, Charlemagne were always pictured with beards!

In our western civilization, there is no general rule about beards. Sometimes they were considered stylish and right for men to have, sometimes no man would want to be seen with a beard!

Long before the conquest of England by the Normans, the beard was considered unfashionable and not worn by men. Then the style changed and beards became popular again! The kings of England, who set the fashions that men followed, varied in their taste for beards. For example, Henry II had no beard, Richard II had a small beard, Henry III had a long beard.

By the middle of the thirteenth century, most men were wearing full and curled beards, and it was common in the fourteenth century. Then beards disappeared again during the fifteenth century, and slowly began to come back into style with the sixteenth century. It was Henry VIII who made the beard fashionable again.

During the time of Queen Elizabeth, lawyers, soldiers, courtiers, and merchants all had beards. But when Anne became queen of England, nobody who was anybody wore either a beard or moustache, or whiskers! In fact, when George III was imprisoned and his beard was allowed to grow, many of his followers felt this was the most insulting thing of all!

So you see that shaving the beard off for a man has not been a question of having a razor. These have existed for thousands of years. To wear a beard or not has been simply a question of style!

---

Today cooking is quite an art. There are great chefs, famous restaurants, thousands and thousands of cookbooks, and millions of people who pride themselves on being able to cook well.

## HOW DID COOKING BEGIN?

Yet there was a time when man didn't even cook his food. The early cave man ate his food raw. Even after fire was discovered, the only kind of cooking that took place was to throw the carcass of an animal on the burning embers.

It was only gradually that man learned to bake in pits with heated stones, and to boil meats and vegetables by dropping red-hot stones into a vessel of water. Primitive peoples used to roast animals whole on a spit over an open fire. In time, people discovered how to bake fish, birds, or small animals in clay. This sealed in the juices and made the food tender. When we come to the ancient Egyptians, we find that they had carried cooking to the point where public bakeries were turning out bread for the people!

Greek civilization advanced cooking to a stage of great luxury. In ancient Athens, they even imported food from distant lands. And the Romans had magnificent banquets in their day!

Then, during the Middle Ages, the art of cooking declined and the only place where fine cooking was found was in the monasteries. When good cooking was revived again, Italy, Spain, and France led the way. These countries prided themselves on having a more refined taste than England and Germany, where the people ate chiefly meat.

A curious thing about cooking is that many primitive peoples knew almost every form of cooking that we practice now. They just did it more crudely. For instance, we cook by broiling, roasting, frying, baking, stewing or boiling, steaming, parching, and drying. Our own American Indians actually knew all these ways of cooking, except frying!

You may think that the chief reason for cooking food is to make it taste better. Actually, the changes cooking produces in food help us to digest it better. Cooking food also guards our health, because the heat destroys parasites and bacteria which might cause us harm.

No matter how good mother's cooking is, we like to go out to a restaurant sometimes (if we can afford it). It's not just because there's different food to eat, but we also enjoy the "going out."

## HOW DID RESTAURANTS START?

Long before there were restaurants, there were taverns where people gathered to talk, have something to drink, and perhaps something to eat.

In London, there was another kind of place that was also the forerunner of the restaurant. This was the cookshop. The chief business of these cookshops was the sale of cooked meats which customers carried away with them. But sometimes a cookshop would also serve meals on the premises and was somewhat like a restaurant. There were cookshops in London as long ago as the twelfth century!

The first place where a meal was provided every day at a fixed hour was the tavern in England. They often became "dining clubs," and these existed in the fifteenth century. By the middle of the sixteenth century, many townspeople of all classes had the habit of dining out in the taverns. Most of the taverns offered a good dinner for a shilling or less, with wine and ale as extras. Many of the taverns became meeting places of the leading people of the day. Shakespeare used to be a regular customer of the Mermaid Tavern in London.

About 1650 coffeehouses also sprang up in England. They served coffee, tea, and chocolate, which were all new drinks at that time. Sometimes they served meals, too.

In 1765 a man named Boulanger opened a place in Paris which served meals and light refreshments, and he called his place a "restaurant." This is the first time this word was used. It was a great success and many other places like it soon opened. In a short time, all over France, there were similar eating places called "restaurants." But the word "restaurant" was not used in England until the end of the nineteenth century.

In the United States, the first restaurant of which there are records was the Blue Anchor Tavern in Philadelphia, opened in 1683.

The name of everything we come in contact with has an origin, and sometimes it's quite surprising to discover how certain names began.

Take a name like gooseberry, for example. It has nothing to do

## HOW DID FRUITS AND VEGETABLES GET THEIR NAMES?

with geese! It was originally gorseberry. In Saxon, *gorst* from which "gorse" is derived, meant "rough." And this berry has this name because it grows on a rough or thorny shrub! Raspberry comes from the German verb *raspen,* which means to rub together or rub as with a file. The marks on this berry were thought to resemble a file.

Strawberry is really a corruption of "strayberry," which was so named because of the way runners from this plant stray in all directions! Cranberry was once called "craneberry," because the slender stalks resemble the long legs and neck of the crane. Currants were so called because they first came from Corinth. Cherries got their name from the city of Cerasus.

The term grape is our English equivalent of the Italian *grappo,* and the Dutch and French *grappe,* all of which mean a "bunch." Raisin is a French word which comes from the Latin *racenus,* a dried grape.

The greengage plum gets its name from Lord Gage, who introduced it into England, and from its greenish color when ripe. Apricot

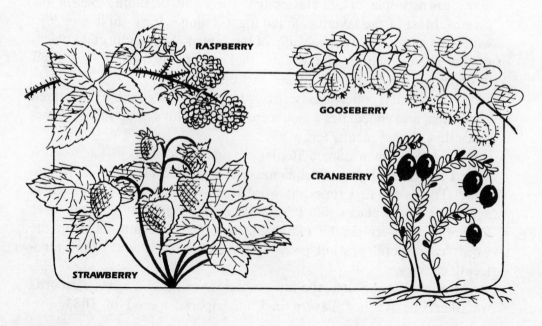

RASPBERRY

GOOSEBERRY

CRANBERRY

STRAWBERRY

comes from the Latin *praecoquus,* which means early ripe. Melon is Greek for apple.

Tomato is the West Indian name for love-apple. The pineapple gets its name naturally from its resemblance to the pine cone. A strange name like pomegranate comes from the Latin *pomum,* a fruit, and *granatus* meaning many seeds.

Chestnuts are so named because they originally came from a city called Castana. Walnut came from the Saxon word *wahl-nut,* meaning foreign nut, since it originally came from Persia. Spinach was *Hispanach,* the Arabic word for a Spanish plant!

---

All over the world today, wherever big cities have grown up, there are very tall buildings that might be called skyscrapers. There is no special reason for calling a building a skyscraper. It's simply a name we have given to very tall buildings.

## WHAT WAS THE FIRST SKYSCRAPER?

In fact, the Bible tells of an attempt to put up a building so tall that it could never be covered by the waters of any flood. This, of course, was the Tower of Babel. During the Middle Ages, the people who lived in the cities of northern Europe began to build great cathedrals. Master builders learned how to fashion stones into pointed arches and flying buttresses to raise ceilings. Tall spires were added to give greater height and majesty to these churches.

For hundreds of years afterwards, these cathedrals stood as the tallest structures in the world. It was simply because no one had discovered materials and methods of construction which could be used to build taller buildings.

In the nineteenth century, as cities grew more crowded, the value of land there rose. In order to make room for more offices on a small plot of land, it was necessary to erect taller buildings. When the hydraulic elevator was invented, it became possible to take passengers and freight as high as 20 stories. But the problem was that to put up a stone building of such height, the walls on the ground floor would have to be more than 7 feet thick to support the weight of the building. So another material was required to make skyscrapers possible.

About this time, three structures were put up that used iron or steel to support great weight with safety. They were the Crystal Palace in London, the Eiffel Tower in Paris, and the Brooklyn Bridge in New York. Architects began to experiment with buildings that had steel frames.

The first skyscraper in the United States was the Home Insurance Building in Chicago, designed in 1883.

---

We are always hearing about how what happens on Wall Street somehow affects the lives of people all over the world. What is actually meant by "Wall Street," and how can it influence the lives of millions of people?

## WHAT IS "WALL STREET"?

Wall Street is literally a street in the lower part of New York City. On it or near it are concentrated the chief financial institutions of the United States. It is, therefore, in a sense, the financial capital of the world. Decisions made here, and activities carried on here influence the economy of our country, and, therefore, touch the lives of all of us in some way.

Wall Street owes its name to Peter Stuyvesant who, in 1652, as Governor of the little Dutch settlement of New Amsterdam, ordered a wall built there to protect the town from attacks by the English. After the Revolutionary War the government offices of the city, of the State of New York, and the United States were located there. President George Washington was inaugurated there in 1789, and the first United States Congress met there.

Today, "Wall Street" indicates the whole financial district, which actually extends several blocks north and south of the street, and also includes an area west of Broadway. In this section are found the headquarters of banks, insurance companies, railway companies, and big industrial corporations. It is also the home of the New York Stock Exchange, which is probably the single most important institution in all of Wall Street.

The securities of about 1,500 different companies producing many kinds of goods and services are traded on the New York Stock Exchange. Within a few minutes after each sale of a stock is made, it is reported to brokerage firms all over the country. These offices receive the information by telegraph on the famous "ticker tape."

---

If you were stranded on a desert island and you wanted to get something from one place to another, what would you do? You would carry it! In primitive times human muscles were the only means of transporting anything. Man was his own "beast of burden."

## WHAT WAS THE FIRST MEANS OF TRANSPORTATION?

In time man tamed certain animals and taught them to carry riders or other loads. The ox, the donkey, the water buffalo, the horse, and the camel were used by early man in various parts of the world for transportation.

This satisfied man for thousands of years, but then he wanted to find some way by which animals could transport more goods. So he developed crude sledges and drags to hitch to his animals.

Flat-bottomed sledges and sleds with runners were fine on snow, but not much good on regular ground. So man developed the rolling drag. This consisted of sections of logs used as rollers under a drag or platform. When the platform was pulled, the logs under it rolled. This made the work easier than pulling the platform along the bare ground. As the platform moved along, it passed completely over the logs at the back. Then these were picked up and put under the front end of the platform.

After a long time, someone thought of cutting a slice from the end of a log and making a hole in its center. This was a wheel, one of man's greatest discoveries. When two wheels were joined by an axle and the axle was fastened to a platform, man had made a crude cart.

Solid wooden wheels were heavy and clumsy, and they wore down quickly. In the course of thousands of years, man improved the wheel. By building wheels with separate hubs and spokes and rims, he made them lighter and more efficient. He made rims and tires of copper or iron so that the wheels would last longer. At last he learned to use rubber tires, and improvements in these are being developed by scientists experimenting with synthetics.

---

The story of mankind has been divided by historians into three great sections—ancient times, the Middle Ages, and modern times. The Middle Ages span the time between the fall of Rome and the beginning of modern times in the fifteenth century.

## WHAT WERE THE MIDDLE AGES?

Of course, when you consider such a great period of time, it's difficult to give exact dates for the beginning and for the end. One age merges gradually into the next. But the date most commonly used as the beginning of the Middle Ages is A.D. 476, when the last of the Roman emperors was dethroned. Its end is usually marked at 1453, when Constantinople, the capital of the Eastern Empire, fell to the Turks.

What was life like during the Middle Ages? What important things happened during this time? This was the epoch during which Christianity triumphed over pagan Europe. In the Middle Ages, the feudal system grew and then decayed in Europe, and the foundations for modern nations were laid.

Although this was the age of chivalry, there was also much cruelty. Lords expressed noble and romantic beliefs in flowery language, but they treated their serfs and slaves with inhumanity.

This was a time when people had unquestioning faith. In no other time did religion play so important a part. The Church and State were not only bound closely together, but often the Church was the State. Towards the end of the Middle Ages, the popes began to lose their power in matters that did not deal with religion.

Modern commerce began in the Middle Ages with the search for new sea routes to India and China.

Science did not make great progress during the Middle Ages, and most of the literature of the time dealt with chivalry and battle. Architecture in the Middle Ages was expressed most fully in the magnificent Gothic cathedrals and their stained-glass windows.

Do you know what the word *renaissance* means? It is the French word for "rebirth." The Renaissance was a period of rebirth that took place in Europe between the fourteenth and sixteenth centuries.

## WHAT WAS THE RENAISSANCE?

During the Middle Ages which preceded it, a great many things in life had been neglected. During the Renaissance, learning was revived. Commerce, art, music, literature, and science flourished. The Renaissance changed the whole way of life in Europe.

Before the Renaissance, most people lived on large estates, called manors. There were few towns or cities. All social life centered in the manor, in the nobleman's castle, or in the bishop's palace. Europe was divided into countless small states, each ruled by a prince or a nobleman.

During the Renaissance, this way of living changed completely. Towns and cities grew rapidly as commerce, industry, and trade developed. Wealthy merchants became important. Instead of numerous small states, larger units of government grew up and became nations. People began to use coined money.

People also began to question their old beliefs. They became more interested in the affairs of this world and less concerned about life in the next. This was when the revolt against the practices and ideas of the Roman Catholic Church took place, which resulted in the Reformation and the establishment of the Protestant religion.

The Renaissance didn't begin suddenly, though sometimes the date for its beginning is given as 1453 when Constantinople fell into the hands of the Turks, or 1440, when printing was invented. The forces that brought it about had been at work for many years before.

The Renaissance reached its height first in Italy before spreading to the other countries of Europe. In Italy there was gathered a great group of brilliant artists, among them Leonardo da Vinci, Michelangelo, Raphael, Titian, Botticelli, Cellini, and others whose work we still admire today.

Let us see what we mean by democracy. The word "democracy" comes from the Greek language and means "rule of the people." As we use the word today, we usually mean a government where the people help to direct the work of the government.

## HOW DID DEMOCRACY ORIGINATE?

Political democracy has appeared

in two general forms. A government in which all the people meet together to decide the policy and to elect the officials to carry it out is known as direct democracy. When the people elect representatives to carry out their wishes, the government is known as a representative democracy. Because direct democracy is not possible on a large scale with many people involved, almost all forms of democracy practiced today are the representative kind.

No nation can be considered democratic unless it gives protection to various human liberties. Among these liberties are freedom of speech, movement, association, press, religion, and equality before the law.

Political democracy began early in history. In the Greek city-states, especially Athens, there existed direct democracy. In Athens, however, the ruling class of citizens was only a small part of the population. Most of the people were slaves, and these, together with women and foreigners, had no right to vote or hold office. So while a form of direct democracy did exist in ancient Athens, we would today find fault with many of its aspects.

Modern democracy owes a great deal to the Middle Ages. One idea of the time was the contract theory. It was believed that a contract existed between rulers and their subjects by which each was required to perform certain duties. If the ruler failed to perform his duties, then the people had the right to take back the powers they had given him.

Modern representation also began in feudal times because of the needs of kings. The feudal monarchs called representative meetings in order to request grants of money. They felt people wouldn't object to new taxes if their representatives agreed to them beforehand. But this helped establish the idea of representation.

---

The concept of justice, or law, comes into being as soon as any kind of social relationship is created. For example, Robinson Crusoe, living alone, had no need for laws. There was no one with whose rights he could interfere by exercising his own freedom of action. But as soon as his man Friday appeared, there was a chance of conflict between his rights and those of his servant. Law then became necessary.

## HOW DID OUR LAWS ORIGINATE?

The purpose of law is to set down and to make clear the social relationships among individuals and between the individual and society. It tries to give to each person as much liberty of action as fits in with the liberty of others.

Laws usually develop from the customs of a people. The earliest known system of laws was formed about 1700 B.C. by Hammurabi, King of Babylon. He set down a code, or complete list of laws, that defined personal and property rights, contracts, and so on.

Customs grew into laws because the force of government was put behind them. Later, laws grew from decisions that were made by courts and from books in which lawyers wrote down what had been learned. Still later, laws were set down in statute books, or codes, by kings and legislators.

The Romans were a great law making people and the law books of Emperor Justinian, who lived from 527 to 565, summed up 1,000 years of their working-out of laws. During the Middle Ages, people's actions were largely governed by the church, which developed a body of laws called canon law.

In the twelfth century, the Roman law began to be studied in Italy and gradually spread to the rest of Europe. Thus, a body of laws, based on the Roman law, developed into what is called civil law, as contrasted with the canon law. At the same time, the courts of England were making many decisions about law, and from these grew up a body of laws called the common law.

In 1804, Napoleon put into a book all the civil laws of his time. This Napoleonic Code is the foundation of the law on the continent of Europe and in Central and South America. The common law system, which developed in England, is the basis of the law in the United States, Canada (except Quebec), Australia, and New Zealand.

---

The supreme law of the United States is written out in the Constitution. It is the one set of laws that everyone — no matter what city or state he lives in — must obey.

## WHAT IS THE BILL OF RIGHTS?

When the Constitutional Convention met in 1787 to draw up the Constitution, most of the delegates took for granted that there were various rights people had that didn't have to be written into the Constitution. But Virginia and many other states felt that it would be wiser to protect those individual rights by having them written down, and so they insisted that a Bill of Rights be added to the Constitution.

Ten amendments, known as the Bill of Rights, were added to the Constitution. The Bill of Rights guarantees that:

1. People have the right to say and write what they wish, to meet together peaceably and to complain to the government. Congress cannot set up an official religion or keep people from worshiping as they wish.

2. The states have the right to arm and drill their own citizens in a state militia.

3. In peacetime, people cannot be forced to take soldiers into their homes.

4. An official cannot search a person or his home or seize his property without a warrant. A warrant (a paper signed by a judge) can be issued only if it is necessary to catch a criminal or to prevent a crime.

5. No person can be put on trial unless a grand jury has decided that there is enough evidence for a trial. No person can be tried twice for the same crime. No person can be forced to give testimony against himself. No person can be executed, imprisoned, or fined except after a fair trial. Private property cannot be seized for public use unless the owner is paid a fair price.

6. A person accused of a crime must be tried quickly; the trial must be public; he has a right to have a jury hear his case; he must be told of what he is accused.

7. In a lawsuit for more than $20, a person can demand a jury trial.

8. An accused person has the right to put up bail.

9. The rights listed here are not the only rights that people have.

10. The powers not given to the federal government nor forbidden by it to the States, belong to the states or to the people.

In these times of world tension, we hear a great deal about the United Nations. What is it? Why was it established? What is it supposed to do? We can give only a brief description of the United Nations here, but here

## WHAT IS THE UNITED NATIONS?

are some things you should know about it.

The United Nations is an organization of governments. It was set up to prevent war and to build a better world for all by dealing with problems which can best be solved through international action. The UN constitution, known as the Charter, was signed at San Francisco on June 26, 1945, by representatives of 50 nations.

According to the Charter, the UN has four chief purposes. The first is to maintain peace by settling disputes peacefully or by taking steps to stop aggression, that is, armed attack. The second is to develop friendly relations among nations based on the equal rights of peoples and their own choices of government. The third is to achieve international cooperation in solving economic, social, cultural, and humanitarian problems. And the fourth is to serve as a center where the actions of nations can be combined in trying to attain these aims.

The UN is divided into six main working groups. The first is the General Assembly. Made up of all the members, each with one vote, it is the policy-making body of the UN.

The second is the Security Council, which is responsible for the maintenance of peace. China, France, Great Britain, the Soviet Union, and the United States have permanent seats and special voting privileges. The other six members are elected by the General Assembly for terms of two years.

The third is the Economic and Social Council with eighteen members. Its job is to promote the welfare of peoples and to further human rights and fundamental freedoms.

The fourth is the Trusteeship Council which supervises the welfare of dependent peoples under the UN and helps them towards self-government.

The fifth is the International Court of Justice which settles legal disputes.

The sixth is the Secretariat, the administrative and office staff of the UN. Its chief officer is secretary-general of the United Nations.

# CHAPTER 5
# HOW THINGS
# ARE MADE

**WHAT WAS THE INDUSTRIAL REVOLUTION?**

Man has been around on this earth for a long, long time. Yet in all his long history, the biggest change in his daily life has taken place in only the last 200 years! This change in the way man lives and works is based on the development of the machine, and is called the Industrial Revolution.

As far back as history goes, man has been making tools. But only after the year 1750 were real machines invented. A machine is like a tool, except that it does nearly all the work and supplies nearly all the power. This change, from tools to machines, was so important and so great, that it began to affect every phase of our lives. In tracing how one development led to another, you will see how this was so.

Before man could make much use of machines he had to harness new souces of power. Before the Industrial Revolution man used only his own muscles, the muscles of animals, wind power, and water power. To operate the new machines he had invented, man developed a new source of power—steam. This made it possible to build factories, and they were built where raw materials were available and close to markets.

As machines were used more and more, a need arose for more iron and steel. And for this, new methods of mining coal were necessary. Then, as machines were able to turn out more and more goods, it was necessary to improve transportation to get them to the markets. This led to the improvement of roads, the building of canals, the development of the railroads, and also the development of large ships to get some of these products to faraway markets.

As men began to do business with markets all over the world, better communication became important. So the telegraph and telephone were developed. But there was a still greater change to come. As factories developed and large and expensive machines began to be used, people could no longer work at home. So men began to leave their homes and go to work in factories and mills. In time this led to the "division of labor," which meant that in a factory a worker did only one job all day long instead of turning out the entire product as he used to do at home.

And finally, the Industrial Revolution made it possible to produce plentiful and cheap goods which everybody could afford.

---

If we were to take the value of all the gold, silver, and diamonds that are mined in one year, it would not equal the profits that are obtained from U. S. patent rights in the same year!

## WHAT IS A PATENT?

What is a patent? It is an agreement between the government, representing the public, and the inventor. The government agrees that no one but the inventor will be allowed to manufacture, use, or sell his invention for a period of 17 years without the inventor's permission. In return, the inventor files his new discovery in the patent office so that everyone may profit from it when the 17 years are over.

The basic principle for granting patents is based on two questions: "Is the invention useful?" and "Is it new?" This principle is now used all over the word in granting patent rights.

Any person who has invented or discovered a new and useful art, machine, manufacture, or composition of matter may obtain a patent for it. This also includes any new or useful improvement.

Application for the patent must be made by the inventor, who is usually guided by patent lawyers or agents. A written description and drawings of the invention, together with an application fee must be submitted to the Patent Office. There are almost a hundred divisions and subdivisions of the office, each covering a different field of invention.

Government patent examiners decide the patentability of the invention. If the examiner refuses a patent, the inventor may appeal his case all the way to the Supreme Court! Once the patent is granted, it becomes the inventor's own property, and he may sell or assign it. The assignment must be recorded in the Patent Office. If anyone disregards a patent, the inventor can force him to stop using it or sue him for the profits made.

The patented article or the package in which it is sold must be marked with its patent number. If it's marked with the word "Patent" when none has been granted, there is a fine of $100 for each offense!

---

No one knows where or by whom the windmill was invented. Probably it was suggested by the sails of a boat.

A boat can sail at right angles to the wind by slanting its sail

## HOW DOES A WINDMILL WORK?

slightly. In the same way, the "fan" or "sail" of a windmill can be driven around in a circle even when placed at right angles to the wind. The windmill is like a huge propeller, with the source of power that turns it coming from the wind instead of a machine.

The first windmills were used in Holland about 800 years ago to drain the flat fields of water. At one time windmills were common in all the flat countries near Holland. The chief use of a mill as we know it is to grind grain. In most countries mills are placed near running streams, a mill dam is built, and the water turns the mill.

But in the flat countries the streams are too sluggish to be used in this way. So windmills are built to grind the grain. In Germany there are mills in which the whole tower can be turned to face the wind as it changes. But in Holland only the roof of the windmill is revolved.

This is done by a small windmill, which is located on the other side of the roof from the big windmill and at right angles to it. When it begins to work, it turns a mechanism which sets the roof moving on little wheels and soon the big windmill is facing the wind.

The fans of a windmill are usually made of wood over which canvas has been stretched. Ropes are attached to the fans so that they can be adjusted if the wind is too strong. The fans are often 40 feet long!

Windmills of an improved type are still used in the United States and Australia. Windmills in the United States are made almost entirely of galvanized sheet steel. Each has a rudder which swings the wheel around on a pivot to catch the wind from every direction. Windmills are especially common in parts of California and in some dry regions of the West. They serve as a cheap source of power for pumping water from wells to irrigate fields, or to water cattle in pastures.

---

A few hundred years ago, who would have believed that millions of people would be working and living in buildings so tall that they couldn't walk the distance to their floors? Huge buildings shooting up into the sky in our big cities would be impossible without the elevator.

## HOW DOES AN ELEVATOR WORK?

The elevator is about 100 years old. By 1850 many three and four story buildings in New York were having hydraulic elevators installed. A cage or platform was mounted on top of a long plunger set in a cylinder. To raise the elevator, water was pumped into this cylinder. To lower the elevator, its operator pulled a switch which released the water in the cylinder. The water was tapped into a tank so that it could be used over and over again.

Today there are very few elevators of this type in use. Not only are they slow, but since the rod that lifts the elevator has to go straight into the ground, they cannot be used in very high buildings.

A certain type of hydraulic elevator is still used in moderately high buildings. It has a shaft, or rod, that is pushed up out of the ground; the rod is not under the platform, but is just beside it. It pushes up one end of a set of pulleys, or blocks, the other end of which lifts the elevator.

It was really the electric elevator which made it possible to put up high buildings. The elevator itself is lifted by a cable which turns on a drum set in the top of the shaft. This drum is turned by an electric motor which is stationed at the top of the building. In the newest elevators the drum has been replaced by a single pulley, which is driven directly by the motor. Through this pulley passes the cable, which is attached at one end of the elevator, and at the other end to a weight which balances the elevator.

Modern elevators have many devices built into them to prevent accidents. One of these is the air-cushion box at the bottom of the shaft. As the elevator sinks into it, the platform fits more and more tightly, so that less air escapes. The result is that an air cushion is formed and the fall is broken gradually. Another safety device consists of two steel balls which spread apart as they turn until they press a brake which stops the elevator.

---

The sun was man's first clock. Long ago men guessed at the time of day by watching the sun as it moved across the sky. It was easy to recognize sunrise and sunset, but harder to know when it was noon, the time when

## HOW DOES A SUNDIAL TELL TIME?

the sun is highest above the horizon. In between these times, it was difficult to tell time by the position of the sun.

Then men noticed that the shadow changed in length and moved during the day. They found they could tell time more accurately by watching shadows than by looking at the sun. From this it was an easy step to inventing the sundial, which is really a shadow clock. Instead of

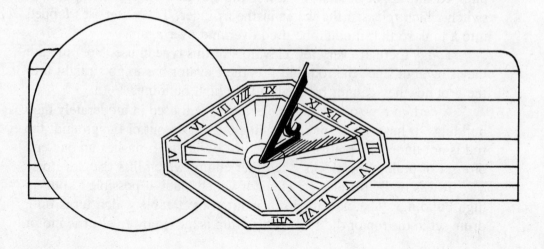

trying to guess the position of the sun and thus the time of day, the shadow gave a more accurate idea of the sun's position.

The first sundials were probably poles stuck into the ground. Stones placed around a pole marked the positions of the shadow as it moved during the day. Thus men could measure the passing of time. Later, huge stone columns were used. Cleopatra's Needle, now in Central Park in New York City, was once part of a sundial. Smaller sundials were used too. One small Egyptian sundial, about 3,500 years old, is shaped like an L. It lays flat on its longer leg, on which marks show six periods of time.

About 300 B.C. a Chaldean astronomer invented a new kind of sundial, shaped like a bowl. A shadow thrown by a pointer moved along and marked 12 hours of the day. This sort of sundial was very accurate and continued to be used for many centuries.

Today sundials are built in gardens for their beauty rather than for their usefulness. However, on the walls and window sills of old houses one sometimes sees crude sundials. They are so arranged that a nail or the edge of the window casing will cast the shadow. In an accurate sundial, the pointer must be slanted at an angle equal to the latitude of the place where it is to be used. A vertical pointer will show the correct time only at one latitude and at one season. If the dial is flat, the hour marks must be spaced unequally on it.

---

Before man discovered fire, the only heat and light he had was provided by the sun. Since he couldn't control this, he was quite helpless in dealing with cold and darkness.

## HOW WERE LAMPS FIRST MADE?

Probably more than 100,000 years ago, he discovered fire. Then he began to notice that some materials burned better than others. Perhaps he observed that fat dripping into the fire from roasting meat burned brightly. As time passed, man began to select materials which, when burned, provided better light. Splinters of certain woods were stuck into the wall and they burned slowly. Pine knots were used as torches. Animal fats were placed in shallow stone dishes and moss and other materials were used as wicks. These were the first oil lamps. Exactly when this happened we cannot know, since it was before recorded history.

The first candles were made by melting animal fats, such as lard and tallow, and pouring the liquid into a mold such as a hollow bamboo. Fibers twisted together were strung through the center so that when it cooled, the solid rod of fat had a wick in the center. Thus, the candle was created at an unknown date long before Christ was born.

Lard was used in lard-oil lamps in New England around 1820. From whale blubber, oil was extracted for whale-oil lamps. In fact, whatever kind of oil was easiest to obtain was used for lamps. Along the Mediterranean there are many olive trees. So olive oil was used for lamps there. The Japanese and Chinese obtained oil for their lamps from various nuts. Peanuts would probably be used for oil for lamps today—if mineral oil in the earth had not been discovered.

Petroleum was discovered in 1859. By heating this oil in a closed vessel, a thin colorless product known as kerosene is obtained. This became the oil most commonly used for lamps. In fact, it was first called "coal oil," because people thought petroleum was associated with coal.

Do you have an oil lamp in your house today? Many homes keep one on hand to use in an emergency if the electricity should fail!

---

It is a curious thing how boys of all times in all countries seem to get the same idea about games. The game of marbles for instance, which is played in every city in this country, has been played all over the world practically since the beginning of history!

## HOW WERE MARBLES MADE?

Nobody knows just when marbles began, but it probably goes back to the first time somebody discovered that a round stone pebble would roll. And that goes back at least to the Stone Age. Scientists have discovered among Stone Age remains little balls which were too small to be used for anything but games.

Long before the Christian Era, children in ancient Egypt and Rome were playing with marbles. In Europe, marbles were played in the Middle Ages. In England the game of marbles developed from a game called "bowls," very much like bowling.

Today, some form of the game of marbles is played almost everywhere in the world. The South American boy called his marbles "bolitas." In China, boys play a game of marbles that involves kicking them. The Persian peasant boy plays with marbles he has made out of baked mud or he uses small stones. Even the Zulus play a game of marbles!

In our own country, boys usually play with two kinds of marbles. They are called "shooters" and "play marbles." Shooters are also called "taws" in some sections of the country. A shooter or taw can not be larger than 3/4 inch in diameter, and it must not be smaller than 17/32 inch. It may be made of either glass, baked clay, agate, or plastic. It is the player's favorite marble which he uses over and over again to shoot at other marbles.

Play marbles, or "mibs," are the marbles at which the player aims his shooter. They are made of baked clay, glass, stone, onyx, marble, alabaster, or plastic. Sometimes the play marbles are named after the material they are made of, such as glassies, clayies, and agates.

Most of the natural baked clay marbles and those of natural onyx come from Ohio. Glass marbles are usually made by melting the glass and, while it is hot, pressing it between the two halves of polished metal molds.

---

We may think of glass as being produced by the mixture of some very special chemicals in a very special way, a sort of miracle of chemistry. But actually, glass is made by a rather simple process using quite ordinary materials.

## WHAT IS USED IN MAKING GLASS?

Glass is a substance made by "fusing" (melting together) certain materials, and then cooling the mixture so that the atoms arrange themselves in an unorganized pattern. What materials? Well, about 95 per cent of the raw materials in the earth could be used in making glass! The most important materials used in making glass, however, are: sand (silica), soda, limestone, borax, boric acid, magnesium oxide, and lead oxide.

Nature herself produced the first glass. About 450,000,000 years ago molten (melted) rock in the core of the earth forced its way to the surface and broke through the earth's crust in volcanoes. When the hot lava contained silica and cooled rapidly, it formed a glass as hard as a rock. This volcanic glass is called obsidian.

Glass has been made by man since very ancient times. The Egyptians, more than 5,000 years ago, knew how to make a kind of colored glass with which they covered stone and pottery and sometimes made into beads. Perfume and ointment bottles made of glass were used in Egypt more than 3,500 years ago.

The Roman Empire (1st century B.C. to 5th century A.D.) was one of the greatest periods in the history of glass. It was at this time that man learned how to blow glass and thus form hundreds of different shapes and sizes of glass objects.

Today, of course, there are many new ways of making glass that have been developed. But this is the basic process. The raw materials for glass are brought to the glass factory and stored in huge bins. The raw materials are carefully measured and then mixed into a "batch." Then broken glass of the same formula, called "cullet," is added to the batch to speed the melting. The batch is fed automatically into the furnace. The glass then flows out of the furnace at lower temperatures.

Then the glass goes through many processes such as blowing, pressing, rolling, casting and drawing—depending on the type of glass that is being made.

---

Glass blowing is one of the oldest of skills. But as modern machines have been developed and perfected, and as the use of glass has increased, glass blowing by hand is becoming rarer and rarer.

## HOW CAN GLASS BE BLOWN?

When glass is in a melted state, it can be "worked" in many ways. It can be blown, pressed, drawn, or rolled. For hundreds of years, the chief method of working with glass was blowing.

The glassworker gathered a ball of molten glass on the end of his blow-pipe and blew, just the way you would blow a soap bubble. Using his skill, he shaped the glass as he blew, and drew it out to the correct thinness. He kept reheating the glass to keep it workable, and then he would finish it with special tools.

In this way, many kinds of glass objects were made. Glass could also be blown into molds and shaped in that way. Surprisingly enough, window glass used to be made by blowing a long cylinder of glass which was split and flattened to produce a sheet of glass. Of course, the size of these sheets was limited by the lung power of the glassblower!

Today, this method of blowing glass (called "freehand") is still used to produce special scientific apparatus and very expensive and beautiful glass articles. But the demand for glass containers such as bottles became so great that efforts were made to create a glass-blowing machine, and finally in 1903 the first automatic machine for blowing glass was invented.

This machine uses a vacuum to suck in a sufficient amount of glass to form each bottle. First the neck of the bottle is molded. Then compressed air is turned on, and the finished bottle is blown. After that, the bottle is automatically annealed, which means it is cooled gradually to make it tough and strong. This machine can turn out more bottles in one hour than six men doing free-hand blowing can do in a day!

Later, another machine was developed for automatically blowing light bulbs, which made possible the wide use of electric light. Most of the world's bottles, jars, tumblers, and other blown-glass containers are made by machine.

---

Can you imagine a modern city without neon signs? This form of illumination and advertising has become so popular that it can be seen all over the world. What is neon and how are the signs made?

## HOW ARE NEON SIGNS MADE?

Neon is a gas. In every 65,000 parts of air there is one part of neon gas. Even though it occurs in such small amounts, neon is taken from the air and used in electric signs.

In 1898, Sir William Ramsay and M. W. Travers, English chemists, distilled liquid air and found a small residue left. This gas they called "neon," meaning "the new." Neon is a gas that has neither color, taste, nor smell. It is one of the "inert" gases. Like helium and other heavier gases, neon will not unite with any other element, and for that reason is found only in the free state.

A neon lamp contains this gas through which flows a current of electricity. As this current, which consists of moving electrons, moves through the gas, the electrons collide with gas atoms and impart some of their energy to the atoms.

Now electrons normally circulate around the nucleus of the atom. But when the collision takes place, some of them are dislodged from their usual positions. Atoms which contain such disturbed electrons are said to be in the "excited state."

After a brief period, the excited atoms lose their extra energy and snap back into their normal positions. Each time this happens, a bundle of light is produced and emitted.

The light that is given off is a reddish-orange glow. Like any other red rays, these rays can penetrate thick fog and atmosphere more easily than other types of light. By adding very small amounts of mercury, a light blue color can be obtained. By using different combinations of rare gases, such as helium and argon, with neon, signs in all colors are possible.

---

Rubber is a sticky, elastic solid obtained from a milky liquid in plants known as latex (not sap). The latex appears in the bark, roots, stem, branches, leaves, and fruit of certain plants and trees. Rubber has been

## HOW DO WE GET RUBBER?

found in more than 400 different vines, shrubs, and trees—though the amount found differs greatly in each case.

The question then is how long ago did man discover that certain plants and trees contained this substance we call rubber? Rubber itself existed millions of years ago. Men have found fossils of rubber-producing plants which date back almost 3,000,000 years! So we'll probably never know exactly when the first primitive man discovered rubber.

We do know that man knew about rubber at least nine hundred years ago. Archeologists have dug up crude rubber balls in ruins of Inca and Mayan civilizations in Central and South America.

As a matter of fact, we might give Christopher Columbus some credit for discovering rubber. A Spanish subject who was with Columbus on his second voyage to the New World, wrote a report in which he told of natives in Haiti playing a game with a ball made from "the gum of a tree."

In 1520, Emperor Montezuma entertained Cortes and his soldiers in Mexico City with a game played with rubber balls. And it is believed that even earlier the natives of southeastern Asia knew of rubber prepared from the "juice" of a tree. They used it to make torches, and coated baskets and jars with it to make them waterproof.

In 1736 a Frenchman named La Condamine sent a report and samples of rubber to Paris from an expedition to South America. He described how the natives made shoes, battle shields, and bottles from the rubber, and how it was used to waterproof clothing. So rubber seems to have been one of man's early discoveries.

---

Like so many other things created by man or produced by nature, chlorine can be both harmful and helpful! In wartime, some of the most terrifying poison gases use chlorine as a base. In peacetime, it is one

## WHAT IS CHLORINE?

of man's most valuable safeguards of health.

Chlorine forms a part of many germicides and disinfectants (substances which destroy germs). Most city water purification systems use chlorine to kill any bacteria that survive after the water has been treated. Only about 4 or 5 parts of liquid chlorine per 1,000,000 parts of water are used for this. This amount is not harmful to humans although the water may sometimes have a chlorinated taste.

Chlorine combines readily with many other elements so that it is not found free in nature, but in compounds. Common salt (sodium chloride) is the most familiar example of this.

Pure chlorine is a suffocating, greenish-yellow gas. It was first prepared by a Swedish chemist in 1774. In 1810 it was recognized as an element by Sir Humphry Davy. It is now obtained cheaply and in large quantities by passing a current of electricity through a solution of common salt.

Chlorine may be liquefied by refrigeration or compressed to a liquid. In that form, it is shipped in iron cylinders or even in specially designed tank cars.

Chlorine is used for bleaching and in preparing bleaching powder. The largest single use is in beaching in the process of making paper. Chlorine is an important part of modern antiseptics and of the anesthetic, chloroform.

In most of the secretions that animals produce in their body, there are some chlorine salts. For example, the gastric juice in the stomach contains an acid formed of chlorine and hydrogen, known as hydrochloric acid.

---

You've probably seen pictures of police using tear gas to break up riots, or to make criminals leave some building in which they have barricaded themselves.

## WHAT IS TEAR GAS?

Tear gas is only one of many gases which have been developed to produce certain effects on the human body so that the victim is helpless or injured, or even killed. It is not pleasant even to think about these gases and their effect, but they are all part of what is considered "chemical warfare."

Choking gases act on the respiratory system, inflaming the lungs. They cause coughing and make it hard to breathe. Blister gases attack any part of the body which they touch, especially moistened parts. They cause burns and destroy tissue. Mustard gas is one of these.

Sneeze gases cause sneezing, intense pain in the nose, throat and chest, and have other strong effects. Blood gases directly affect the heart action, the nerve reflexes, and may interfere with the breathing in of oxygen. Carbon monoxide is one of these gases.

Nerve gases cause nausea, twitching of the body, and may result in death.

Tear gas irritates the mucous membrane around the eyes, causing intense smarting, a flow of tears, and makes it impossible for a person to see clearly. In its original form, tear gas is a sugarlike solid material. When it is heated it forms a vapor that attacks the eyes. Tear gas is placed in grenades and paper projectiles and fired through the windows into the room where the criminal has taken refuge. The white cloud of tear gas soon blinds him so that he gives up. The effect of tear gas is only temporary. As soon as a person leaves the contaminated area he recovers.

But it isn't only in war or against criminals that poison gases must be considered. Gasoline engines throw off a poison gas called carbon monoxide, which is why automobiles must not be run in closed garages!

---

Tar seems to be such a simple ordinary thing, yet few products have had a history that can match it in importance or excitement!

When people first began to heat coal to get coke for furnaces, the

**WHAT IS TAR?**

stiff black liquid that came from it was thought valueless. It was coal tar and it was thrown away. Today, more than 200,000 by-products are made from coal tar—products that we use every single day of our lives!

The first use of coal tar was as a fuel. Later on, it was used as a protective coating on wood and ropes. Finally it was discovered that other useful substances could be made from the tar. When the tar was heated and distilled, different oils were obtained. One of these was used as a substitute for turpentine.

Then in 1856, a 17-year-old chemistry assistant in England, William Henry Perkin, accidentally discovered that certain dyes, called aniline, could be made from coal tar. This opened a whole new world of industry.

How are various products obtained from coal tar? It is done by the process of distillation. The tar is boiled in big ovens that have bent tubes leading from them. The gases and liquids that are given off are collected. Coal tar itself contains a little of everything. As it is distilled again and again, different substances are drawn off. The pitch that remains is the tar we are familiar with in tar shingles, tar-paper roofing, and in asphalt for paving streets.

What are some of the by-products of coal tar? Most of the colors now used for dyes and printing inks are made from coal tar. Carbolic acid, used as antiseptic in hospitals, comes from coal tar. Aspirin comes from coal tar. Saccharin, which is 550 times as sweet as cane sugar, is a coal-tar product. The entire modern plastics industry is based on coal tar. Nylon is a combination of coal, air, and water. Clothing and textile fibers are being made from coal today.

Mothballs, artificial flavors, and soda water are coal tar products. Chemicals made with the help of coal are used in food. So you see that in a lump of coal, and in the tar which comes from it, we have the source of thousands of products we all use every day.

The love of perfume is probably as old as the human race. Vases containing oily pastes that were still fragrant have been found in Egyptian tombs 5,000 years old.

## HOW IS PERFUME OBTAINED FROM FLOWERS?

The Arabians were the first to distill rose petals with water to produce rose water. This was 1,200 years ago. Today, there are two chief methods used to extract the perfume from flowers. One that is widely used is called "enfleurage," which means enflowering.

In this method, sheets of glass are set in wooden frames. They are coated with purified lard and covered with flower petals. Then they are stacked one above the other. The flower petals are replaced at intervals until the pomade, as the purified lard is called, has absorbed the desired amount of perfume.

A more modern method is to extract the perfume from the flower petals with a very pure solvent obtained from petroleum. This solvent is repeatedly circulated through fresh petals until it is saturated with perfume. The solvent is then removed by distillation and the perfume purified with alcohol.

Flowers are only one of the sources of perfume essences. There are cedarwood and sandalwood, cinnamon bark, myrrh, and the various aromatic resins and balsams. There are many leaves such as rosemary, lavender, patchouli, peppermint, geranium, and thyme. The rinds of the orange, lemon and lime, as well as the roots of orris and ginger, are also used. Among the great families of flowers especially famous for fragrance are roses, violets, jasmine, orange blossoms, tuberoses, and jonquils.

Very few perfumes on the market today are pure floral essences. Most of them are a blend of small quantities of natural flower essences with animal and synthetic materials. Chemists are now even able to make beautiful floral scents which would be very difficult to obtain in nature.

---

If you've ever gone out on a picnic or had a barbecue in your back yard, you've probably used charcoal for cooking the food. Charcoal gives a hot fire with very little smoke or flame.

## WHAT IS CHARCOAL?

But charcoal has many other important uses too. It has a part in making gas masks, water filters, pencils, polishes, tooth pastes, and medicines. What is charcoal? It is a black, spongelike substance left when animal or vegetable material is partially burned. It is almost pure carbon.

It may be made from wood or from animal bones by heating or burning them in such a way that the water and gases contained in them are driven off and the solid material is left. The charcoal which is made from bones is called "bone black." It is very useful as a filtering agent, because it absorbs impurities, coloring material, and bad odors.

Lamp black and ivory black are used in making printing inks and as a pigment in oil paints. Lamp black is the soot obtained by burning resin, turpentine, tar, oil, or fats with a limited amount of air. Ivory black is made from waste chips of ivory.

Wood charcoal is usually made in one of two ways. The first method consists of covering piles of wood with dirt or sods. Then a fire is built at the bottom of the pile and the wood is allowed to burn slowly, or char. This method has been followed for hundreds of years in the forests of northern Europe. It is wasteful because it makes no use of the gases which keep escaping during the process.

In the second method the wood is piled into iron buggies. These are pulled or pushed into huge ovens, called "retors." When the fire is burning brightly, it is partially smothered by closing the draft. The wood gradually turns to charcoal. The escaping gases are collected in another chamber and valuable substances such as wood alcohol and acetic acid are condensed from them.

Since wood charcoal is a poor conductor of heat, it is also used as an insulator. It is used in gas masks because of its power to absorb gases. And sticks of charcoal made from willow wood, are used by artists and art students for drawing.

---

Milk is considered to be the nearly perfect food. It supplies the body with proteins, with a form of sugar (lactose), minerals, and vitamins.

Years ago most people used to drink milk just about as it came

## HOW DO WE PRESERVE MILK?

from the cow. Today milk is treated in various ways for many reasons. Some of these are health reasons. Some are for convenience.

Milk is evaporated in order to preserve it. Evaporated milk has had about one half of the water in it removed. It is made by heating the milk in a vacuum to evaporate the water without overheating or scorching the milk. The thickened milk is canned, sealed, and sterilized.

The food value of evaporated milk with an equal amount of water added, is about the same as the food value of whole pasteurized milk. When evaporated milk is sealed in the can and sterilized, it can be stored without refrigerating it. You can see what a great convenience this is under certain conditions. Once the can is opened, however, evaporated milk needs the same care as fresh pastuerized milk.

Another form of preserved, or concentrated, milk is sweetened condensed milk. It is milk evaporated to about half its volume to which sugar has been added. Sweetened condensed milk is not sterilized. It depends on the sugar in it for preservation.

One of the most widely used ways to preserve milk is to dehydrate (or powder) it. In dehydration, water is removed from milk and only the dry milk powder is left. The most common method of making dried or powdered milk is the spraying process. The milk is first evaporated. The thickened milk which is left is then forced as a fine spray into a large drying chamber. Blasts of hot air quickly absorb the moisture from the milk spray. The milk powder falls to the bottom of the drying chamber. It is then removed and packaged.

Powdered milk is changed to liquid milk by adding water. Nine pounds of water added to one pound of milk powder make it taste like whole milk.

---

It would be hard for us to imagine life without soap. Staying clean is such an important need, that most of us would think soap was one of man's first discoveries. Yet soap was absolutely unknown until the

## HOW DOES SOAP CLEAN?

beginning of the Christian Era. So man has had soap for less than 2,000 years!

Soap is made by the action of alkali on fats or oils. In simple terms, when these are boiled together, soap is produced. The alkalies used are usually soda and potash. How does soap clean?

There are several ideas as to how this happens. One is that soap breaks the greasy dirt into particles so small that the water can wash them away. They become emulsified, or like a milky liquid, with the water and are easily rinsed away.

Another idea is that the soap lubricates the dirt particles, making it easier for the water to remove them. In other words, the soap makes the dirt so slippery that it can not hang on the surface to which it has been attached. Water has what is called a surface tension; that is, it behaves as if it were covered with a thin, elastic film. This surface tension keeps the water from getting in and under and around small particles of dirt, soot, and dust on the skin and in soiled fabrics. Soap dissolved in water is supposed to lower this surface tension so that the soapy solution can surround the dirt particles and pry them off, making it easy to flush them away.

Soaps and other cleansing agents are often called detergents. This comes from the Latin word detergere, which means to wipe off. Many people think that a detergent is not a soap, but actually, soaps as well as special cleansing agents can be called detergents.

Modern chemistry has created powerful cleansers that are special "wetting agents." These are sometimes called "soapless soaps." The special ability of these to clean is due to the way they break down the surface tension of water. They are thus able to penetrate especially well under all kinds of dirt. Wetting agents are used in shampoos, washing powders and in toothpastes.

There are many kinds of soap made for special uses. Scouring soaps contain abrasive material. Naphtha soaps contain naphtha for cutting heavy grease. Saddle soaps have a little wax which remains on the leather when dried. Castile soap is made with olive oil.

---

Do you know of any candy that is not sweet? As a matter of fact, people sometimes refer to candy as "sweets." This is because the most important part of all candy is sugar.

## WHEN WAS CANDY FIRST EATEN?

Now that we know this, it will not surprise us to learn how the word "candy" came into being. In Persia, about the year 500 A.D., they were able to make sugar in solid form. The Persian name for white sugar was "kandi-sefid." And that's where we got the word "candy!"

In ancient times, most people had something that could be considered a sort of candy, even if they didn't have sugar. The Egyptians, for example, have left written and picture records of candy and candy-making. But since they didn't know how to refine sugar, they used honey as a sweetener. And they used dates as the basis for their sweetmeats. In many parts of the Far East, even today, each tribe has its official candy-maker and secret recipes. They use almonds, honey, and figs to make their candy.

Oddly enough, nobody in Europe had the idea of making something sweet to eat for its own sake until quite recently. They would use sweet syrup to hide the taste of bitter medicines. Then, in the seventeenth century, a great deal of sugar began to be shipped to Europe from the colonies. So candy-making as a separate art began in Europe at that time.

The French were the first to candy fruits and to develop their recipes. One of these, a nut and sugar-syrup sweet called prawlings, may have been the forerunner of the famous New Orleans pralines.

The early American settlers boiled the sap of the maple tree to make maple-sugar candy. Taffy pulls were social events, and sugar crystals were grown and formed on strings to make rock candy. About 1850 small lozenges, many of them heart-shaped, had romantic messages printed on them. Later on, candy shops began to sell peppermint lozenges and chocolate drops, and the candy business was on its way!

Did you know that Napoleon had a great deal to do with the development of canned food? Of course, people had been trying for thousands of years to find better ways to preserve food for a long time. But it was

## WHEN DID THE CANNING OF FOOD START?

Napoleon, during his military campaigns, that really gave canning a start.

The French soldiers and sailors who were fighting Napoleon's wars often had to fight on a diet limited to smoked fish, salt meat, and hardtack. Thousands of men died from scurvy and slow starvation. So, in 1795, the French government offered a prize of 12,000 francs for the most practical method of giving French armies and navies fresh and wholesome food. Fifteen years later, the prize was awarded to Nicholas Appert, a chef and confectioner who lived near Paris.

What Appert did was to pack the food into wide-mouth glass bottles. Then he sealed the bottles with cork and wire, and put each bottle into its own cloth sack for protection. He next lowered the bottles into a boiler filled with hot water. A lid was put on, so that the bottles would heat in their boiling water bath.

Appert's method is as effective today for some foods as it was then, although the theory upon which he worked was not correct. He thought it was only necessary to keep out air to preserve cooked food. Later it was learned that preserving canned food depends on absence of invisible bacteria.

The first patent for a "tin canister" for preserving food was granted in England to Peter Durand in 1810. He got the idea from the canisters in which tea was packed. In America, the name was shortened to "tin can," and we call this industry "canning," while in England it is known as "tinning."

The first cannery in the United States was one for fish, and was started by Ezra Dagget in New York City in 1819. The next year, fruit preserves and tomatoes were put up in glass in Boston.

To can a food successfully, it must be heated enough to kill the organisms (molds, yeasts, bacteria) that may cause fresh food to spoil; the tin can or glass jar must be free from germs, and it must be sealed air-tight.

For some reason, Americans have not become as fond of tea as the people of other countries. In the United States, we use only about a pound of tea a year per person, but in England it takes nine pounds to satisfy their needs!

## HOW IS TEA PROCESSED?

The Chinese, of course, are the world's original and greatest tea drinkers. They have enjoyed tea for more than 4,000 years! It was only about 300 years ago that Europeans first tasted tea.

The tea bush, or tree, actually doesn't grow wild in China, so it is believed that the Chinese themselves imported the first seeds from India. When the British came to India and discovered tea, they began to establish large plantations there and in Ceylon. In time, more tea was exported from Ceylon than from China!

There are two main varieties of tea plants. The Chinese kind grows only three or four feet high, while the Indian plant can reach heights of 20 feet. Tea leaves, if they are not picked, can grow to the size of a man's hands. But since small, tender leaves make a better grade of tea, the tea plants are usually pruned. It takes a tea bush three years to produce its first crop, and that's only half an ounce of tea!

Next to the tenderness of the leaf, the next most important quality about tea is the altitude at which it is grown. The best tea comes from high mountain plantations. Once the leaves are picked, they are carried to the factory where the curing process has to begin immediately.

The leaves are spread over shelves to wilt. Then they are passed into rolling machines, which free the juices. Black and green tea leaves come from the same plant. When black tea is desired, the rolled green leaves are spread out again and covered with wet cloths. This makes the leaves ferment and change to a blackish color. Afterward the leaves are dried, sorted, and then packed for shipment. The best black tea is orange pekoe, which is made from the youngest and tenderest leaves of the plants.

Oolong tea, which is a favorite in this country, comes from Formosa. It is neither green nor quite black, since it is only partly fermented.

The reason tea is stimulating is that it contains caffeine, just as coffee does. Another substance in tea is tannin, which sometimes makes the tea bitter.

It would be natural to assume that clothing originated because of the desire of man to protect himself from the weather. Yet, actually, this was only one of the reasons.

## HOW DID CLOTHING ORIGINATE?

Equally important was the desire of people to make themselves attractive in the eyes of other people. Primitive man spread colored clays over his body for this purpose. Later on, as he invented knife blades of bone, flint, and stone, he slashed his skin and rubbed colored clay into the cuts. This was the beginning of what we call tattooing.

As time went on, primitive man found other methods of gaining attention. He would suspend trophies of battle and hunting from his body, such as strings of teeth and bones. Around his waist he hung the skins of animals, pieces of horn, feathers, scalps, and the like. Later the necklace was replaced by a tunic or shirt and a skirt was added to the waistband.

The next step in the development of clothing was the actual covering of the body with some sort of material. Soon this was worn not only for adornment, but for protection and modesty.

When the glacial periods came, and snow and rain fell, a naked tribesman would seek shelter in the cave of some wild beast, perhaps a bear. If he could find a live animal, he killed it. Then, he made a hole in its body, crawled inside and slept until the carcass was cold. Then he flayed off its skin and wore it by day and slept in it by night.

In this way the furs and skins of wild beasts became the clothing of man. These early hunters invented the art of sewing. They used sharp-edged knives for skinning animals. They made awls of flint for boring holes in which to insert thongs to bind the cloth together. The most important part of their inventions was the needle with an eye.

Needles with eyes, buttons, and clasps have been found in Stone Age caves of central Europe and the Swiss villages of 30,000 to 40,000 years ago! Some needles that are very long were made from the leg bones of large birds. Others were made of ivory and are fine enough to sew almost any garment today! In some parts of the world, grasses and leaves were tied, interwined, and woven together into clothing.

The making of clothing was thus one of the first arts developed by man.

---

Of all the fibers used in making cloth, cotton is the most important. It is the world's chief material for clothing. There are good reasons for this. Cotton is cheap, it has a natural twist which makes it easy to spin

## WHAT IS COTTON?

into thread, it needs no special preparation, it washes well, and it is strong.

Cotton has been used by man for more than 3,000 years! It was known to the people of India and China long before Europe found out about it. In fact, when Europeans first learned of cotton, they described it by comparing it to wool, and for a long time it was even called "cotton wool." At first, cotton was very expensive and only the rich could afford it. When Columbus tried to reach India, one of the treasures he hoped to find was cotton.

Cotton grows on a plant which reaches a height of about 3 or 4 feet. When the flowers first appear they are creamy white, and they turn pink later. Then the pod, or boll, appears and in about 6 to 9 weeks the boll ripens, turns brown, and bursts open to reveal the soft white fibers. The fibers are long hairs which grow out of the seed coats.

Cotton picking means picking the ripe bolls from the plant. This has to be done with great care, in order not to injure the unripe bolls on the plant. After the cotton is picked, it is loaded into wagons and hauled to a nearby gin, where it goes into a ginning machine. A cotton gin (short for "engine") removes the seeds from the cotton fibers. Before Eli Whitney invented the cotton gin, it took a man an entire day to remove the seeds from one pound of cotton! A modern gin can clean several thousand pounds of cotton a day.

After being ginned, the cotton fibers are pressed into bales weighing about 500 pounds each, and shipped to the textile mills, where it is manufactured into cloth. Cotton cloth may be as flimsy as gauze for bandages or as strong as fabrics for making canvas tents and awnings. When it is waterproofed it may be used in making umbrellas and raincoats. Cotton is one of the most versatile fabrics known to man!

---

There is an old French word *boton,* which means a "bud." And this word probably came from a still older word *bouter,* which means "to push out." Our word button comes from these words, because this is exactly what a

## WHEN WERE BUTTONS FIRST USED?

button does. It sticks out from whatever it is attached to, ready to be pushed out through a buttonhole or loop to fasten articles together.

Nobody knows by whom buttons were first used, or when. They go back to the beginning of history; some experts say to 30,000 or 40,000 years ago! Yet a funny thing about buttons is that in some parts of the world they have never been used. After all, think of all the ways there are to fasten clothing and keep it in place: pinning, buckling, lacing, belting down, wrapping around and draping, and tying together!

Another thing about buttons is that sometimes they go out of style for clothing and are not used for long periods of time, perhaps hundreds of years. From the time of the ancient Romans until almost the end of the Middle Ages, buttons were not worn by people in Italy, Spain, and France!

In the fourteenth century, buttons became popular in Europe and from that time on they have never gone entirely out of fashion. Buttons have been made from almost any kind of material you can imagine. Metal buttons have been made of gold, silver, steel, copper, tin, aluminum, nickel, brass, pewter, and bronze.

Animal products have been used for making buttons and these include: bone, horn, hoof, hair, leather, ivory, and shells! In addition, buttons have been made from cloth, thread, paper, glass, porcelain, rubber, wood, sawdust, oatmeal, peach pits, and birds' feathers!

At one time, men and boys wore buttons for jewelry. In 1685 King Louis XIV of France ordered many diamond buttons for himself, including one set of 75, each costing more than $200.

---

Tartan is the name for a woolen cloth woven in a pattern of crossbars. These bars are of a certain width and color for each pattern of tartan, and are the same in both directions. A distinctive pattern for tartan is called a sett.

## WHY DO THE SCOTS MAKE VARIOUS TARTANS?

The different setts of tartan get their names from the clans. In ancient days in the Scottish Highlands, life was organized into clans. The people living in a certain district put themselves under the leadership of a chief for protection. The title of chief remained in the same family, and the name of the chief's family became the name of the clan.

The Highlanders made their clothing from the wool of sheep which grazed on the hillsides. This wool was colored with native vegetable dyes and was woven into garments. Gradually the different clans began to adopt certain colors and patterns to set themselves apart. Since these clans frequently waged war on each other, their tartans served as a uniform, and showed membership in a special clan.

In time, other types of tartans developed. A hunting tartan was adopted to have suitable colors for blending with the countryside. District tartans were worn by people who didn't belong to any clan. The clergy developed its own sett.

Before the eighteenth century, a tartan was worn as a garment about five feet wide and six yards long. It was worn with the lower half draped around the waist and held by a belt. The upper half was draped over the belt, brought around to the back, and fastened at the left shoulder with a pin. Later, this garment was cut into two pieces. The lower half became the kilt, and the upper half the plaid. Plaid, by the way, does not mean tartan, it refers to a garment worn like a shawl.

To crush the Scottish national spirit, the English Parliament passed laws in 1746 abolishing the clan system, prohibiting the playing of bagpipes and the wearing of kilts and tartans. These laws were repealed in 1782, and after that the kilt and the wearing of the tartan came back into fashion among the Scots. But now it has become a national costume, and is kept for special occasions.

The making of leather is one of the oldest industries. Even before man began to make rude axes and spears, he must have wrapped himself in the skins of animals to keep off the cold and the rain.

## HOW WAS LEATHER FIRST MADE?

Since ancient man usually hung his skins over the fire to dry, he found that smoke preserved the hides. Later he found that the wood and bark of certain trees preserved skins even better than smoke. He also removed the hairs.

When recorded history began, man was making almost as good leather as that which is made today. Pieces of leather made by the Egyptians as early as 3000 B.C. are still in good condition. The Babylonians and the Hebrews knew ways of making leather which are almost the same as present processes.

Sometimes the leather was preserved by tanning it with the bark of trees, sometimes by curing it with salt, and sometimes by rubbing it with oil. The American Indians made especially fine leather by cleaning the hair and flesh from the hides, dressing the hides with oil, and finally smoking them.

Like the people of today, the ancients found leather one of the most useful materials. Much of our knowledge of ancient nations comes from records written on parchment, which was made from the skins of sheep, goats, and calves. Leather was used by soldiers for helmets, shields, and jackets. It served sailors as sails and coverings for ships. Bottles, rugs, shoes, and even coins were made of leather.

Hides of cattle form one of the chief sources of leather, but the skins of many other animals are also used. As a rule, the skins of larger animals, such as cattle, buffaloes, or elephants, are called hides, while those of smaller animals are simply called skins.

Among the animals whose skin is used for leather are calves, pigs, horses, sheep, goats, deer, ostriches, alligators, lizards, snakes, seals, whales, sharks, and walruses.

---

Early man who lived where sharp rocks hurt his feet, soon began to think of some way of protecting them. So he made a mat of woven grass, or used a strip of hide or a flat piece of wood as a "sandal." He

## HOW WERE SHOES FIRST MADE?

fastened these to the bottom of his feet with thongs cut from hide. Sometimes these thongs were brought between the toes and tied around the ankles. In colder parts of the world, man soon felt a need to give the foot even more protection, so he added more material to the top of the sandal, and thus the shoe was born.

Sandals were worn by the ancient Egyptians as long as 5,000 years ago! At first, in fact, the sandals were worn only by the rich Egyptians. They would walk along followed by a servant who carried a pair of sandals, just in case the master would need or want to put them on. Later of course, all the people began wearing them. Sometimes they made the sandals with upturned toes, to give the foot more protection. Egyptians were the first shoemakers in the world.

The Greeks developed the boot by gradually changing the straps which held the sandals to the feet into solid leather. Even today many primitive forms of shoes still survive. We still wear sandals very much like those worn by ancient Romans and Greeks. We have moccasins which are like those worn by the American Indians. And people in Holland still wear wooden shoes!

Modern shoes as we know them began to appear in the Middle Ages about the time the Crusades started. Because the Crusaders went on long journeys they needed good protection for their feet, and so people began to make shoes that would last for a long time.

In time shoes became an object of fashion and all kinds of ridiculous styles appeared. At one time it was the fashion to wear long-toed shoes, with toes six inches long coming to a sharp point! These were so uncomfortable that they had to be abandoned, so another new fashion was invented—the high heel.

In America, a shoemaker named Thomas Beard arrived on the second voyage of the Mayflower in 1629, and his little shop was the start of our great shoe industry.

---

The reason photography is possible is that light acts a certain way on a chemically prepared substance. This substance is called the emulsion and it coats the film which is used in taking a picture.

## HOW IS CAMERA FILM MADE?

When light strikes the chemical silver nitrate it turns black. So the first step in making film is to obtain silver nitrate crystals. The film is prepared somewhat the way a piece of bread is spread with jam. The "jam" is the emulsion on the face of the film, with the "seeds" representing silver particles or grains which are sensitive to light. The "bread" is the flexible, transparent plastic base. The main parts of the emulsion are the silver particles and gelatin.

The first step in making the film itself is to mix gelatin with silver nitrate and potassium bromide in a warm, syrupy form. This must be done in total darkness because the silver crystals are sensitive to light. The nitrate and potassium combine as potassium nitrate, and this is washed away. Silver bromide crystals are left in the gelatin. This is the emulsion.

The film itself is made by first treating cotton fibers or wood pulp with acetic acid. This makes a white flaky product called cellulose acetate. The cellulose acetate is then dissolved and the mixture forms clear, thick fluid known as "dope."

The dope is fed evenly onto chromium-plated wheels. As the wheels turn, heat drives off the solvents, and the dope becomes a thin, flexible, transparent sheet. Next, the film base is coated with the emulsion. The dry film is then slit into proper widths and wound into spools.

When a picture is taken, light strikes this film. When this happens, the tiny silver bromide grains inside the film emulsion are exposed. They become, in the developing process, the dark part of the film negative from which positives, or prints, are made.

191

One of the most beautiful ways to decorate a church is to fill the windows with designs in stained glass. In addition to providing decoration, the designs usually illustrate the Scriptures.

## HOW ARE STAINED GLASS WINDOWS MADE?

No one knows when stained glass was first made. It probably started in the Near East, the home of the glass industry, about the ninth century. Before that time glass wasn't made in a great variety of colors. The first reference that can be found to stained glass as we know it (which means not just colored windows but windows that tell a story) goes back to the year 969, and tells about such windows being installed in the cathedral at Reims, France. The oldest stained-glass windows still in existence are from the eleventh century.

In the design of a stained-glass window, six things play a part in the composition: (1) the glass containing color as a stain; (2) small details such as the features of people, which are painted on the glass with brown pigment; (3) lead strips which hold the pieces of glass together; (4) iron T-bars which support the leaded glass in sections; (5) the tracery of stone or wood which divides the window itself; (6) round iron "saddle" bars, which are fastened across the glass to take the wind pressure. So you see that designing a stained-glass window is not like painting a picture. All these elements have to be considered by the designer in creating his effect.

To make a window, the designer makes full-sized drawings first. This shows each piece of glass and its color, and all the elements listed above. He then cuts pieces of glass to fit the drawing. Then each piece that requires paint is painted, and these are fired in a kiln which turns the paint to an enamel. Then the pieces are leaded together and the whole design is put into place.

The dominant color in stained-glass windows is always a primary one—red, blue, or yellow. In old stained-glass windows it was always a rich red or blue, which made the windows quite dark. Later, more yellow was used to admit more light.

---

Silver is one of the most widely distributed of all metals. About 2,000,000 tons of it float about in solution in the sea, but it would not pay to get it out. In the main, silver comes only in ores from which it must be separated.

## WHAT IS STERLING SILVER?

In this ore, silver is usually combined with sulphur as silver sulphide, or is a part of other sulphides, chiefly those of copper, lead, or arsenic. Silver therefore has to be separated from these sulphides to obtain it in pure form.

But silver is too soft to be used in its pure state. That's why silver coins contain 90 per cent silver and 10 per cent copper. The sterling silver of which jewelry and silverware are made, contains 92.5 per cent silver and 7.5 per cent copper.

The name "sterling" comes from a German family named Easterling. The absolute honesty of the Easterlings as traders persuaded King John of England (in 1215) to give them the job of making the English coins. They did it so well and truly that their name is still used as a sign of solid worth. All sterling silver is stamped with a hallmark—either the word "sterling," or a symbol, varying in different countries. The English symbol is a lion.

Many people in former generations, although they wanted sterling silver, could not afford it and they welcomed the invention of Sheffield plate. To make this, a sheet of copper and one of silver are rolled together so that the silver completely hides the copper. This fine plated ware was made in Sheffield and Birmingham, England, and was not cheap. To reduce the cost still more, a thin layer of silver may be coated on any desired metal object by electroplating. Silverplate is widely used in our country and elsewhere. Silver is also used in many ways in industry.

Hundreds of things we use every day are objects that have been electroplated. The metal decorations on cars have been chromium-plated. Knives and forks and spoons may be silver-plated. Other things around the house may have been copper-plated.

## WHAT IS ELECTROPLATING?

Electroplating is the process of putting a coating of metal on an object through the action of an electric current. The purpose of electroplating is usually to give a metal better appearance, or protect it against corrosion. Sometimes it is for reasons of health, as when the steel for food cans is tin-plated.

In order to electroplate an object, three things are necessary. First, a supply of direct electric current. Second, a piece of pure metal. And third, a liquid which contains some of the metal to be used in plating.

Let's see if we can follow the remarkable process that takes place in electroplating by imagining that we are going to plate a bolt with copper. We take a glass jar or beaker and put in a solution of water and copper sulphate. We thus have a liquid which contains the metal to be used in the plating.

Now we put in a piece of pure copper, and this is attached by a wire to the positive pole of a battery, which is our source of direct current. Now we put in the bolt which is to be plated, after it has been thoroughly cleaned. The bolt is attached by a wire to the negative pole of the battery.

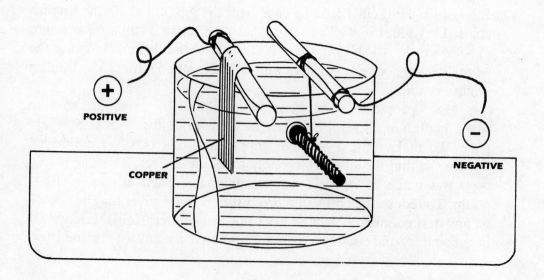

POSITIVE

COPPER

NEGATIVE

When the current flows, an interesting thing happens. The bolt becomes negative, because it is attached to the negative pole of the battery. As you know, electrical opposites attract each other. So the negative bolt attracts the positive part of the copper sulphate and it pulls the copper out of the solution. This copper coats or plates itself on the surface of the metal bolt!

But this is only part of the story! The sulphate which is left in the solution has a negative charge. So it is attracted by the positive charge of the piece of pure copper we put in. When it reaches the copper, it pulls off enough copper to make a molecule of copper sulphate again. So our solution remains as before . . . copper sulphate. In this way, the piece of copper is slowly dissolved and added to the surface of the bolt until it is copper plated. This process, but using different metals and solutions, enables us to beautify or protect metals by electroplating.

---

There was a time when bows and arrows were the chief weapons man had to defend himself against his enemies. They were also the way he earned his livelihood. With bow and arrow he hunted wild game, which supplied him with food, shelter, and clothing.

## WHO INVENTED THE BOW AND ARROW?

Nobody knows who made the first bows and arrows because they go back so far in history. They were probably first used in the Stone Age. We have found drawings thousands of years old on the walls of caves which show archers drawing their bows. There are also ancient arrowheads made of flint which have been found in many parts of the world.

During the Middle Ages, archery was developed to a high degree in England and France. Many of the most important battles and wars in history were waged with bows and arrows as one of the chief weapons. Willam the Conqueror won the Battle of Hastings by having his archers shoot their arrows high into the air so that they would drop upon his English enemies.

Archery, which is the use of bows and arrows, is associated with many of the romantic tales we all know, such as the adventures of Robin Hood, and the story of William Tell. In fact, most of the stories of old England include some mention of archery contests.

Both bows and arrows have to be made with skill and care, using special woods. Usually the bow is made from yew, which comes from Italy, Spain, and the west coast of America. A really good bow is made of one piece of wood. For men, the bow is from 5 feet 8 inches to 6 feet in length. It has a pull, or draw, of from 36 to 80 pounds, so you see it takes a bit of strength to use it. For women, the bow is smaller, about 5 feet to 5 feet 6 inches in length, and its pull, or draw, is only 18 to 35 pounds.

Arrows are usually made from spruce, Norway pine, or a special kind of cedar wood. They have a tip, usually of steel, at one end, and a "nock" at the other. Just below the nock are three feathers, which help steady the arrow in its flight. For men, the length of the arrow is 28 inches, and for women, 24 to 25 inches.

These modern bows and arrows are used chiefly in the sport of archery, but there are many people who hunt deer, bear, and other large animals in this way today!

---

If an atom is so tiny that it cannot be seen, how can it be "exploded?" And how can this explosion create bombs so terrible that they are the most powerful weapons known to man?

## HOW IS AN ATOM "EXPLODED"?

What we are really talking about when we talk about an atomic explosion—is energy. Energy comes from matter. Energy and matter are the two things that make up everything in the universe and keep everything going.

Matter is made of atoms, and every atom has in it particles of energy. Energy holds the parts of an atom together. This energy is so tremendous, that if it can be set free it supplies enormous force. For example, the energy released by exploding one pound of uranium (uranium-235) is greater than the energy released by burning 2,600,000 pounds of coal!

How do we get the atom to release its energy? We have to get to the core of the atom, which is the source of the energy. We do this by splitting the atom. This process is called "fission."

How is it done? By bombarding the atom with neutrons from other atoms. A neutron is a particle within the atom. But this doesn't happen when you bombard just any atoms. In some cases, only a small amount

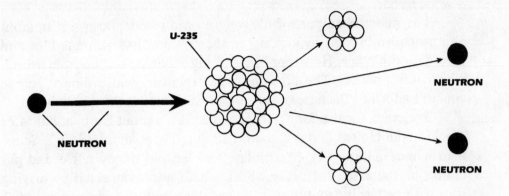

U-235

NEUTRON

NEUTRON

NEUTRON

of energy is released. But when uranium-235 is bombarded by neutrons, a great amount of energy is released.

But that energy is from only one atom. Suppose we could get many atoms to release their energy at one time? This is done by producing what is called a "chain reaction." By having a certain amount of uranium-235 as the target, and bombarding it with neutrons, we would have this happening: as one atom of uranium-235 split and released some of its neutrons, these neutrons would strike the core of another atom. This would release more neutrons which would split more atoms, and so on. In a fraction of a second, a tremendous amount of energy would be released and we would have an "explosion."

This, of course, is a very simplified explanation. But it gives you an idea of how we obtain atomic energy.

Nobody knows who first had the idea for making a vehicle on two wheels on which a person could ride. But some such vehicle did exist as long ago as the days of ancient Egypt! It had two wheels and was set in motion by the feet of the rider.

## WHO INVENTED THE BICYCLE?

The bicycle as we know it began to be developed in the nineteenth century. In 1817 Baron Karl von Drais, a German, introduced into England a machine which he named the draisine, after himself. It was a development of an earlier invention by a Frenchman, J. N. Niepce, and was a real forerunner of the modern bicycle. The two wheels of the draisine were connected by a wooden bar.

The rider rested part of his weight on a wooden arm rest in front and propelled himself by kicking on the ground, first with one foot and then with the other. He steered by turning a handle on the front wheel, which was pivoted. The machine was expensive and ordinary people couldn't afford it. Because of this, they nicknamed it the dandy horse.

The craze for the dandy horse spread throughout Europe, but after reaching the United States it soon died out. Then, about 1840, a Scotsman named Kirkpatrick Macmillan took an old dandy horse and put cranks on the axle of the rear wheel. These were connected by driving rods with pedals in front. But little was done with this invention.

The name "bicycle" was first used in 1865. At that time, a Frenchman, Pierre Lallement, attached cranks and pedals to the front wheel of a velocipede, much like the dandy horse. These "bicycles" were called "boneshakers," for they had heavy wooden frames and iron tires and it was quite an experience to ride them. In 1868 light metal wheels with wire spokes and solid rubber tires were introduced.

The modern "safety bicycle" was developed about 1885. It had two wheels of equal size, and the rider's seat was slightly forward of the rear wheel. The pedals were attached to the frame in a convenient position and power was transmitted from them to the rear wheel by sprockets and the chain.

---

When we think of some of the great tunnels that exist in the world today, we might imagine that the tunnel is a modern invention. But surprisingly enough, tunneling is one of the oldest types of engineering!

## HOW IS A TUNNEL BUILT?

Ancient peoples not only built tunnels but were very expert at it. Among those who built tunnels thousands of years ago were the Egyptians, the people of India, the Assyrians, the Greeks, and the Romans.

Of course, building a tunnel today is quite a different kind of operation than it was in ancient times. Modern equipment makes it easier and safer, and more rapid.

Engineers usually divide tunnels into two classes—those through rock, and those through earth. One of the greatest advances in tunnel building was the invention of the tunneling shield by Mark Brunel, an English engineer. This device made under-water tunneling safe.

The modern tunneling shield is a cylinder of steel, which fits into the head of the tunnel being built. At the front edge of the cylinder is a strong cutting edge. The shield is pushed forward through the earth by powerful jacks.

Men dig out the earth within the front part of the cylinder, while other men build up the lining of the tunnel within the rear part of the cylinder. Where necessary, compressed air may be used to withstand pressure at great depths.

The first step in building a tunnel is to make a geological survey to find out the best route. After the size and shape of the tunnel have been decided, the center line for the tunnel is laid out on paper. The beginning and end are marked on the ground. Then the actual work of tunneling begins.

---

Thousands of years ago, great barriers of earth or stone were built across the Nile River in Egypt and the Tigris River in Babylon. They were built to control the floods of these rivers and to store water for irrigating crops.

## HOW ARE DAMS BUILT?

Today dams are built in all countries. They range in size from small embankments to great engineering works which require the labor of thousands of men and heavy machinery.

In modern construction, concrete has taken the place of stone masonry. Dams up to about 300 feet high are built of earth or rock, in addition to concrete. Higher dams are almost always built of concrete.

A safe dam must rest on a sound foundation and against firm abutments at the ends. However, the foundation immediately under the base of the dam is not always solid rock. Sometimes dams have to be built on overlying material which may be gravel, sand or other earth layers. Such layers are made watertight by means of a steel, concrete, or clay wall.

In all dams some sure means must be provided to care for surplus water after the reservoir behind the dam is filled. This may be accomplished by a spillway, or a concrete overflow, or through openings built through the body of the dam.

The stability of a dam depends on sheer weight, so certain types of dams are called "gravity" dams. In their simplest form, gravity dams are roughly triangular in cross section. Earth and rock dams have sloping faces both upstream and downstream, whereas masonry and concrete gravity dams have their upstream face nearly vertical and a sloping face downstream. The triangular face gives a broad base to resist the over-turning force of the water against the dam.

The very largest and highest modern dams are always of the solid concrete gravity type. When they are built in a straight line across the river, they are called straight gravity type; when built on a curve, they are called arch gravity type.

One of the most remarkable feats in the history of engineering is the building of the Panama Canal. It has had an effect on the commerce of the whole world. For example, it not only shortens the distance from

## WHY DOES THE PANAMA CANAL HAVE LOCKS?

many Atlantic to Pacific ports by 8,000 miles, but it cuts the distance from Great Britain to New Zealand by 1,500 miles.

Originally, the canal was going to be built by the French. The plan called for a canal at sea level, 29½ feet deep, and 72 feet wide at the bottom. But the French plan couldn't be com-pleted for many reasons, and the United States undertook to build the

The French were going to cut below the level of the sea from ocean to ocean. But this plan had its dangers. If the tide happened to be higher at one end than at the other, a dangerous current might result. It also required much more digging. So a lock canal was decided upon. That

THE GATUN LOCKS

meant that there must be water available at the higher levels to fill the higher parts of the canal. This was obtained by damming the Chagres River.

The locks form a kind of "staircase" for taking ships through the canal. This means the ships are raised at certain points to where the water level is higher, and then lowered to other levels. Nearly half of the canal runs through Gatun Lake. Vessels approaching the lake from the Atlantic side are lifted to the lake level, a distance of 85 feet, by a series of three locks. Near the Pacific side is the Gaillard Cut, about 8 miles long. Vessels are then lowered 31 feet in one lock. A mile farther on two more locks lower them another 54 feet, to sea level. Within the locks, the vessels are hauled by electric locomotives moving along the banks. Locks have now been built which are capable of handling the largest ships afloat.

---

Today you can pick up the telephone and in a few minutes be speaking to someone on another continent. Or you can give your telegraph office a message and in a short time a person anywhere in the world can be

## HOW WAS A CABLE LAID ACROSS THE OCEAN?

reading it! Without the cables that lie at the bottom of the oceans, linking all the continents together, this would be impossible.

The first problem that had to be solved in connection with cables was to insulate wire so that electricity would not escape. After many experiments, various materials were discovered that could be wrapped around the cable to insulate it.

Then men began to lay cables, connecting various points. In 1841-42, a telegraph cable was laid under New York harbor. In 1850 the English Channel was spanned by a submarine telegraph cable. A little later, Scotland and Ireland, Sweden and Denmark, and Italy and Corsica were joined by cable.

Finally, in 1857, Cyrus W. Field and an English scientist, Lord Kelvin, tried to span the Atlantic Ocean from Newfoundland to Ireland with a submarine cable. This was quite an undertaking and there were many disappointments before success was achieved. The United States and British governments loaned two warships for the job. Each ship carried half the cable. It was spliced in midocean and then "paid out" as the ships steamed to opposite shores.

The cable broke several times while being laid. Finally, on Aug. 13, 1858, the first message crossed the ocean by means of this cable. But the cable worked for only three months before it burned out. The electric current was too strong for the insulation. No attempt was made to replace the cable until 1865, by which time Lord Kelvin had invented a telegraph instrument which didn't need such a strong current.

The "Great Eastern," then the world's largest ship, was fitted out to lay the cable. The first cable broke about two thirds of the way across from Ireland. In 1866 another cable was laid which reached Newfoundland safely. Then the broken end of the lost cable was found and spliced to another piece, and so there were two cables working. A new age in communication was born.

The largest of all musical instruments is the pipe organ. Sometimes, in smaller models, you can see the rows of pipes over the keys, but a large pipe organ usually is built as part of the building with the pipes and most

## HOW DOES A PIPE ORGAN WORK?

of the machinery hidden away. In the largest organs, there may be as many as 18,000 pipes!

The pipes produce the tones—the big ones the deep heavy tones, the small ones the higher tones. Pipes in a large organ may range from as large as the trunk of a tree to as small as a lead pencil.

The pipes are arranged in groups, and each group is controlled by a stop. When the organist wants to use a particular group of pipes he opens the proper stop. This connects that group with the keyboard.

A large organ may have as many as five rows or banks of keys. Each row is connected with a particular set of pipes. When the organist presses down a key, this moves a valve which lets air into a certain pipe.

These rows of keys, incidentally, are called "manuals" because they are played by the hands (from the Latin word *manus,* meaning "hand"). Since each manual controls a group of pipes, it really controls an organ of its own. The most important manual is called the "great" organ, and the others are called the "choir," "swell," and "solo" organs. The fifth manual, which some organs have, controls the "echo" organ.

The sound produced by the pipes is caused by the air which rushes through them. This air is forced into them from an air chamber into which it has been pumped by a great bellows. This is done today by a blower driven by a motor that may have from 25 to 40 horsepower. But long ago it was necessary to use manpower to operate the bellows. There was an organ in Winchester Cathedral, England, that had a bellows so big it needed 70 men to pump it!

# INDEX